Communication Skills
for the
Foreign-Born Professional

The Professional Writing Series

This volume is one of a series published by ISI Press®. The series is designed to improve the communication skills of professional men and women, as well as students embarking upon professional careers.

Books published, in press, or in preparation for this series:

Communication Skills for the Foreign-Born Professional
  by GREGORY A. BARNES

The Art of Abstracting
  by EDWARD T. CREMMINS

How to Write and Publish a Scientific Paper
  by ROBERT A. DAY

How to Write and Publish Papers in the Medical Sciences
  by EDWARD J. HUTH

How to Write and Publish Engineering Papers and Reports
  by HERBERT B. MICHAELSON

Communication Skills for the Foreign-Born Professional

GREGORY A. BARNES

Philadelphia

Published by

iSi PRESS® A Subsidiary of the
Institute for Scientific Information®
3501 Market St., University City Science Center, Philadelphia, PA 19104 U.S.A.

Library of Congress Cataloging in Publication Data

Barnes, Gregory Allen.
  Communication skills for the foreign-born professional
  (The Professional writing series)
  Bibliography: p.
  Includes index.
  1. English language—Text-books for foreigners. 2. English language—Business English. 3. English language—Technical English. 4. Communication. 5. Professions—United States. I. Title. II. Series
  PE1128.B322   808'.042   82-6148
  ISBN 0-89495-013-4   AACR2
  ISBN 0-89495-014-2 (pbk.)

Printed in the United States of America

Preface

This book was developed for, and out of, a continuing education course of the same title launched at Drexel University in 1980. Its purpose is to give foreign-born professional people, most of whom will speak English as a second language, an understanding of the surprising variety of skills needed to perform successfully in a professional role. Only some of these skills are linguistic; others are nonverbal, cognitive, "compensatory" skills which have equal importance for effective communication.

To address these needs, I requested and received much assistance from specialists in relevant fields. Colleagues in English as a Second Language who have contributed are Professors Alexis Finger and Benkt Wennberg of Drexel University, Carol Puhl of Delaware Technical and Community College, and Barry Taylor of the University of Pennsylvania. Individual chapters were reviewed and criticized by numerous faculty members in Drexel's Department of Humanities and Communications: I thank Professors Deborah Andrews, Thomas Brown, Philip Buehler, Richard Burian, Miriam Kotzin, Michael Markel, and Ralph Most. Department Chairperson Martha Montgomery contributed material support, and colleague Stephen Mandell moral support.

Individual chapters were also read by Drexel colleagues John Gregory, Director, Instructional Systems; Richard Binder, Humanities and Social Sciences Librarian; and M. Claire Schofield, Director of the Reading Clinic. I appreciate their willingness to share their expertise. Four other members of the Drexel faculty went to some trouble to provide materials now in the book as object lessons: Professors Peter Arfaa (Architecture), Joseph Lambert and Joseph Mullin (Civil Engineering), and Lester J. Stradling, Jr. (Mechanical Engineering). Graphics assistance was promptly and cheerfully provided by Deborah Weber and Peter Groesbeck.

Those responsible for stimulating the project also deserve acknowledgment. Dean Samuel Mercer and Director Robert Ross of the Drexel Continuing Education Division encouraged me to develop a course for foreign-born professionals, and their staff—especially Delorea Banner, Lisa Barnett, Marjorie Fromnic, Betty Traub, and Ed Walsh—have helped in many ways to make the course run smoothly. I also appreciate the support of Stanley J. Gwiazda, Dean of the Drexel Evening College, and his staff, in my English as a Second Language duties. Maga Kaminski, Lee Endicott, and Delorea Banner typed the manuscript, and I thank them all.

Finally, I thank my wife, Professor Sandra T. Barnes, who brings not only her anthropological training but also unsentimental editorial skills to my work; and our daughter, Roby, and son, Stephen, whose tuition bills unfailingly encourage me to meet publishers' deadlines.

A Note to the Reader

In writing this book, I have made a number of assumptions about its readers. First, these readers are probably beyond the age of the usual classroom learner. They have focused on a career rather than on the educational process, except possibly education at master's or doctoral level.

Second, I have assumed that they are professionally trained, and are employed, or expect to be employed, in professional roles. Thus, they need to read technical materials, they must write occasionally or even frequently, and they must be ready to give oral presentations to superiors and colleagues.

My third assumption is that they (1) work or study in North America, (2) work with Americans or other native English speakers, or (3) hope to pursue career interests in an English-speaking environment. Thus, effective communication in English is not merely desirable but necessary for the advancement of their careers. For example, one of the skills they need is an ability to deal with the "culture" of English-speaking professional people.

Finally, I have assumed that they already speak English well and read it very well. This book has been written in a plain style (partly so that they may study it on their own); because they read English well, however, I have been able to use the vocabulary necessary to explain various processes which aid the development of professional skills.

My overall assumption is that my readers are both ready and motivated to improve a number of their communication skills, only some of which are "English," or linguistic, in nature. In the Introduction, I outline the strategies for effecting this improvement.

For Coral Windsor and Roby Gregory Barnes

Contents

Chapter 1

Introduction

Communication is the principal function of the professionally trained. The manager has more to do than add up profits and losses; the engineer and architect must do more than design processes or structures; the scientist cannot simply peer into test tubes. The first task of these and other professional people is, rather, to exchange ideas.

Communication depends first—but not exclusively—on language. In the professional world of North America, and indeed of much of the modern world, a mastery of English is essential to the advancement of both individual careers and professional tasks. Thus, those who speak English as a second language may feel that an inability to speak like a native is their major handicap.

Fortunately, their belief is only half correct. If they have begun to speak English on a daily basis only as adults, they are not likely to become flawless speakers. If, however, they master communication skills which are only partly or not at all linguistic, they can succeed in the way that so many "foreigners" or "immigrants" have.

In this introductory chapter, we look first at the problems in language-learning and then at the variety of "compensatory" communication skills which stand outside of language.

Learning a Second Language

Language is our greatest achievement. Every child, brilliant or dull, masters the grammatical complexities of his or her mother tongue with little apparent effort. Some children master a second or even a third language with the same astonishing rapidity.

As we know from hard experience, however, the adult does not learn a second language so easily. The reason is not yet known with certainty. Perhaps the adult's superior ability to reason is a handicap rather than an

1

asset. Language, it seems, is best learned inductively (that is, by imitation and practice of all the items in a language) rather than deductively, or through the application of broad principles.

In physical terms, the difference in the child's and the adult's ability to learn is probably caused by the maturation of the brain. Recent research has shown that the child gradually assigns functions to one side of the brain or the other. Once the process is complete, the brain loses the plasticity, or flexibility, needed to acquire a new language perfectly.

The age at which we lose this plasticity is apparently about 12, although it may happen even earlier. Thus the 10-year-old arriving in the United States may learn to speak English like a native, whereas the 16-year-old will likely retain a slight accent. The adult learner should expect to have, and to keep, an accent (although not all do). The cause of the adult's problems is interference: The system of sounds in the native language interferes with the speaker's ability to produce English sounds. Naturally, interference from Japanese is different from interference from Spanish. Thus, we speak of a Japanese accent, a Spanish accent, and so on.

In America, it has been said, everyone is a foreigner, and the same is true of many other English-speaking countries. Accordingly, accents are common, well tolerated, and even enjoyed. A larger problem is English grammar—for example, verb tenses and word order—where mistakes can cause the native speaker to misunderstand the nonnative speaker. The difficulty is even greater in writing; readers can't "hear" an accent in a written report, but they will see faulty grammar and perhaps be confused.

Unfortunately, the native language interferes with the second language in grammar areas, too. A major example in English is the articles: *a(n)* and *the*. Speakers of languages which have articles of their own (like German or French) may have little trouble with these words. Speakers of Korean or Vietnamese or the many other languages without articles, however, may never learn them perfectly.

Many other grammatical elements will prove almost as difficult. We want to say things, in the new language, the way we say them in our own language, but in fact, our own language interferes. In German, for example, the way to say "He has eaten too much" is *"Er hat zu viel gegessen"* ("He has too much eaten"); therefore, a German translating directly would create an awkward English sentence.

What can foreign-born professional people do to improve their English, then? It may seem discouraging to realize that high intelligence is not enough. The brilliant adult probably will not learn English as quickly as a child of ordinary ability. Nevertheless, there are certain other factors which affect language learning.

First, it is helpful if the adult learner speaks English in several environments, including the home. If the learner's family speaks only the native language, there is little chance that he or she will master the large vocabulary of household terms. Sometimes children force adults to speak English at home, usually with benefit to the adults.

Other environments in which various levels and kinds of English are spoken include social gatherings with native English speakers, sporting events, shopping expeditions, airplane trips, and many more. Neither the classroom nor the work situation is sufficient to give the learner a mastery of English. It is necessary for adults to seek out other environments.

Thus, our social habits in a second culture are important in language learning. The best advice is to be active, be social, talk to native speakers. Assertive people tend to be good language learners; that is, people who know what they want, and intend to get it, will not worry about mistakes in English or the reactions of others. It follows that shyness is not a helpful characteristic in language-learning. When learners are uncertain of themselves, they become inhibited and are afraid to speak out.

Nonnative speakers sometimes lose their inhibitions when they are angry or excited, because at such times they *must* speak. Temporarily, they may be fluent. These situations cannot happen frequently, however. At the other extreme—and surely, this is a happier solution—they speak well when they are completely relaxed. Tests have shown, for example, that drinking a glass of beer or wine often results in improved English— for the nonnative, *not* the native, speaker.

Naturally, nonnative speakers cannot change their personalities in order to learn English. (Nor can they drink a glass of beer before entering each new English-speaking environment.) But they can assign themselves outings; they can go shopping, visit museums, see movies, and talk to their neighbors. They should also force themselves to speak without worrying about correct grammar. This too is important: Making mistakes is natural, and even necessary, if learners are to discover the way to communicate effectively.

Finally, we come to motivation, which may be the most important consideration in language-learning. In any field, we learn well if we want to learn. This seems to be as true of language-learning as of any other discipline, perhaps more so. If we do not want to learn a language thoroughly, we probably will not; if we are strongly devoted to learning it, we probably will.

In short, it is helpful to *like* English, and even to like the language-learning process. And one further point: It usually helps if one likes native speakers and feels a part of the host culture. This raises a serious problem of identity. Few people can turn easily from the chief sources of their identity, which are their own culture and language. Again, it may be more than can be expected of nonnative learners.

Nevertheless, learner motivation is the appropriate concept on which to end a discussion of ways to learn better English. Some scholars believe that language aptitude, or ability, is indeed little more than strong motivation. Certainly, teachers of English, and books on language-learning, will fail unless learners adopt a positive attitude.

"Compensatory" Skills

Whereas the child learns intuitively (without reasoning), the adult learns cognitively, or through analysis. Cognition means "knowing"; adults want to know both *what* and *why*. They look at language-learning and communication as problems to be solved by a systematic approach.

Accordingly, adults make progress most rapidly in the cognitive skills of communication. We have seen that pronunciation is not such a skill. Neither is vocabulary, in most respects, and this is an important point for language-learners to understand. Many such learners believe that, if they can master all the words in a language, they will know the language. That is, they want to attack English as they would harvest a field of corn, row by row.

Unfortunately for them, English has about 650,000 words. Some of the words, such as conjunctions and transition markers, are more important than others; some words, such as prepositions, serve necessary functions but cannot be easily defined or translated; and many words (e.g., the verb "get") have several meanings. Certain function words (those which show the relationship between ideas) will be presented here, but in general, vocabulary needs to be learned in context, and through practice.

Among the strictly linguistic skills, only grammar can be approached analytically, at least in a book of this nature. Certain grammar points, such as the construction of relative clauses, do permit us to apply general rules to hundreds of cases. Appendix III ("Grammar Handbook") at the end of this book works on the most important of these points, first by identifying sentence parts, and then by demonstrating sentence faults which occur when the parts are used incorrectly.

Many other communication skills are strictly, or partly, cognitive. Communication through behavior is an example. Such acts as gestures, the use of space, our way of dressing—acts collectively known as "body language"—are culturally based means of communication. What we have learned in our own culture may be re-learned, cognitively, in our encounter with a new culture. Part I, accordingly, deals with several areas of nonverbal communication used in speaking situations.

Part II moves to the written word and introduces reading skills which only adults can master. To read in English, of course, one must know English. To read *effectively*, however, one needs to apply reading theory to practice, to look for writers' signals, to determine relationships between ideas, to summarize—in short, to perform functions which are mastered by analysis.

Effective writing utilizes even more cognitive skills, and thus the writing process takes up a large part of this book. Part III deals with basic writing principles, and Part IV addresses special problems in writing for the professions; in addition, Appendix II covers the mechanics (e.g., punctuation) of formal writing. Content, organization, manuscript conventions, visual materials—all these attributes, if given proper attention, will compensate for a writer's language problems.

A term used in this book for cognitive communication skills is, in fact, "compensatory skills." The method of the book is to offer a thorough introduction to each skill, and then, at the end of each part, a reading list of works for further study. The presentation of skills is also supported by the exercises for Chapters 2 to 15 presented in Appendix I. Through systematic review and analysis of these materials, the reader can indeed learn to communicate effectively in the English-speaking professional world.

PART I

VERBAL AND NONVERBAL COMMUNICATION

OBJECTIVES

- To discuss public behavior as a means of communication
- To provide suggestions for speaking effectively to groups
- To review modern aids to technical presentations

Our first "compensatory" skills are part of a general subject which usually fascinates those who have lived abroad: communication through behavior. Native English speakers have a culture, as well as a language, different from that of nonnative speakers. They hold their bodies differently, use their eyes differently, and perhaps even eat their food differently.

Within the English-speaking world, moreover, there are many cultures and subcultures. The reserve of the Englishman is foreign to the Californian, and the frequent smiles of the Georgian seem odd to the native of Vermont or Canada. It is therefore difficult to generalize about the culture of any one nationality. How do we define an American, for example?

A few "American qualities" can be identified, perhaps. First, Americans consider themselves democratic, so that each person expects to be treated as an equal by other people. Second, they are independent: They expect to make many personal decisions without interference from their families, their communities, or their government. They are also mobile: An Easterner is prepared to move to the West Coast if a good job is available there. And they are generally competitive, because of a strong belief that they can create better lives for themselves.

Foreign-born visitors do not always admire these characteristics, and they sometimes criticize other "American qualities." To people of other cultures, for example, Americans may seem incapable of deep friendships. Furthermore, they allow their children too much liberty, they don't respect their elders, and they worry too much about clean bodies and clean bathrooms. Perhaps worst of all, they are always in a hurry.

Most people who have worked in the United States recognize these basic traits of American culture. Our concern here, however, is not general customs in the United States; rather, we will look at the customs of a special subculture—that of working professionals. The point is to remind the reader of certain kinds of behavior which will lead to success in professional life.

Thus, in Chapter 2, we discuss ways to behave in social situations, and in Chapter 3, ways to behave in addressing an audience. Chapter 4 is more specialized, for it deals with the technical presentation, a "speech act" which requires the use of audiovisual aids. Today, however, such aids are important means of nonverbal communication in the English-speaking professional world.

Chapter 2

Rules for Social Behavior

We are all prisoners of our cultures. Moreover, we are usually unaware of the laws our cultures impose on us. Although we know how to behave toward a superior, how to hold a job, and how to treat a member of the opposite sex, we cannot state the rules for our behavior; we have learned them unconsciously.

This chapter attempts to state five sets of rules which govern social behavior in the English-speaking professional world. The first has to do with attitudes toward time and the use of time. Almost every visitor knows that native English speakers, particularly Americans, are unusually time-conscious. Less well known—but perhaps a greater cause of misunderstandings—is the set of rules governing personal space. There are also rules for dress and hygiene, for carrying on conversations, and for forming good working relationships.

These are certainly not the only "laws" which govern behavior among professionals, and some will apply more to Americans than to other English-speaking peoples. They are chosen because, generally, they are the most useful in gaining colleagues' friendship and respect.

Time

The careful organization of time is the basis for industrial and technological productivity. England, Canada, Australia, the United States—all of these native English-speaking cultures have benefited from their mastery of the clock and the calendar. So strong is the value placed on time, particularly in America, that schedules and timetables may even control social life.

There are differences between "business time" and "social time," however.

Business time. The rule here is simple: Never be late. When an appointment or a meeting is set for 11 a.m., the professional arrives between 10:58 and 11:01; if he or she arrives after 11:03, an apology is necessary. Similarly, when a report is due on January 15, it is wise to have it ready on January 14. If it will not be ready by January 15, the professional calls on January 14—or on January 8—to explain why.

Naturally, these rules are relaxed among colleagues who work together closely. Nevertheless, the nonnative colleague should not break the rule; let the natives do it. And when reporting to a superior, the professional never arrives late (although the superior will, sometimes). Note too that the superior, or a new acquaintance, wants to get down to business quickly; probably his or her desk calendar is full of appointments.

Generally, English-speaking professionals do not engage in long greetings or extended casual conversation. This does not mean that they are unfriendly. They simply believe that time is valuable, and there are so many things to do.

Social time. The emphasis Americans give to time in social activities strikes foreigners as extreme. Many Americans, for example, believe church services should start promptly at 11 a.m. and end by 12:00; ministers have been dismissed for preaching too long. School dances must end at 10 p.m., even though the boys and girls are behaving themselves and having a wonderful time. Restaurants are sometimes judged by the speed of their service, rather than by the quality of their food.

Different rules exist for informal social gatherings, however—that is, for cocktails, dinners, or parties at people's homes. Here the first rule is: Do not arrive early. The hosts need time to get ready. It is polite to arrive 10 to 15 minutes late for small gatherings, and perhaps 20 minutes late for a large party.

When do visitors leave? The clock is less important here than the actions of the host and hostess. An offer of coffee late in the evening is one sign that they feel the party should end, or one of them may yawn, indicating a desire to go to bed. The first departure of a guest is also a signal to other guests that it is time to leave.

Space

Anthropologist Edward T. Hall, whose books are listed at the end of this part, reports that Americans sometimes find Arabs aggressive ("pushy")—and that Arabs may feel the same way about Americans. One problem seems to lie in the differing cultural conceptions of space. Arabs stand "too close" to Americans; Americans who walk or drive past Arabs "cut in" rudely.

Both Americans and Arabs consider their actions proper, of course. Thus, cultural habits in the use of space cause misunderstandings and suspicion. It follows that foreign residents must adjust to the way English speakers use space, even though English speakers themselves are often unaware of these requirements.

Hall identifies four dimensions of space: intimate (for people loving—or fighting—each other); personal (for informal conversations); social (for work relationships); and public (for strangers). Although the distances he gives (for example, 1 to 4 feet in the "personal" dimension) apply to Americans, they are generally true for all English speakers. It is important at this point to study Figure 1.

Personal distance. English speakers generally avoid body contact when speaking to each other; usually they will not even touch each other with their hands. When they are forced to stand close together, as in an elevator, their muscles tense, they avoid eye contact, and they fall silent. Even husbands and wives generally do not touch in public.

FIG. 1. *Personal space. The man in the middle may stand this close to the woman because he isn't facing her. Note, however, that he has his hands behind him, to avoid touching her. The other man, facing the woman, stands at the outer limit of personal space. If he were farther back, he would be considered impolite.*

English speakers, in fact, have comparatively large "space bubbles"—amounts of space which they expect others to leave them. They do not want to feel the heat of another person's body, to smell another person, or to have another person spray them with saliva during conversation. When other people come too close, they back away, pull their heads back, fold their arms across their chests, or try to put barriers between themselves and the people speaking to them. They are not being cold or impolite; they are simply following the rules of their culture.

The same rules govern distance between a man and a woman as between two people of the same sex. The rules are also about the same for seated people and standing people; English speakers are often uncomfortable sitting, however, when someone standing speaks with them. Finally, the person who stands too *far* away (more than 4 feet) is seen as cold or rude.

Social distance.   Different cultures use home or office space in strikingly different ways. Hall reports, for example, that the Japanese leave the edges of a room bare, whereas Americans leave the center bare. He adds that Americans leave office doors open, Germans close office doors, and British professionals often have no offices.

On the whole, English speakers share space well in a work situation. The boss leaves his or her office door open so that a secretary can walk in or a visitor can look in. A closed office door would suggest that the boss had something to hide. Outside the office, even a messenger is free to walk any corridor or sit down in an empty chair.

Yet there are rules. American men do not like to work closer than 4 feet apart. When they work together at a table or desk, they will sit across from each other and draw their chairs back to converse. On the other hand, two colleagues would not usually sit at opposite ends of a long table, for talking from a distance of more than 7 feet is not polite office behavior. Women, in fact, may sit together at a corner of the table, or even work side by side.

One interesting insight into American culture, and particularly into American office behavior, concerns the question: How does one enter the boss's office? The person who stands in the doorway, or barely enters the room, is considered too timid or deferential. The person who hurries in and rushes too close is considered too aggressive. The "proper" behavior is to walk in firmly and stop about 2 feet from the boss's desk.

Public space.   How close to a stranger may one stand or sit in the street or in a hotel lobby? The rule here is, not close at all. English speakers are uncomfortable when a stranger sits down next to them in a public library or restaurant, if there are plenty of seats elsewhere. If one knows the person, but not well, it is polite to nod or say "Hello"—but not to stand or sit closer than 7 feet, unless the other person begins a conversation.

Grooming

Every culture has its standards for personal attractiveness. Nigerians think plumpness is attractive, whereas Americans prefer slenderness. In France, a man looks attractive wearing a suitcoat over his shoulders, with his arms out of the sleeves; in America, the same man dressed this way would look effeminate. Some peoples like natural body smells; others, including American professionals, do not.

The standards of dress and personal hygiene—known as "grooming"—also vary within the English-speaking world. The British professional dresses differently from American professionals of the Midwest, and no one else dresses like the California movie producer. The standards discussed here are those of the professional world in the northern United States.

Hygiene.   Americans' concern with health and cleanliness is the subject of an amusing article by Horace Miner, an anthropologist. Pretending to write seriously of the "Nacirema" culture, he calls American bathrooms "shrines" where important rituals take place. "The focus of this activity," he writes, "is the human body, the appearance and health of which loom as a dominant concern. . . ." On the matter of oral hygiene, he reports as follows:

> The Nacirema have an almost pathological horror of and fascination with the mouth, the condition of which is believed to have a super- natural influence on all social relationships. Were it not for the rituals of the mouth, they believe that their teeth would fall out, their gums bleed, their jaws shrink, their friends desert them, and their lovers reject them. ("Body Ritual Among the Nacirema," p. 11 in James P. Spradley and Michael A. Rynkiewich, eds., *The Nacirema*, Boston: Little, Brown and Co., 1975)

The reader should understand, of course, that many Americans would not find the article humorous. They believe that all people should bathe daily, brush their teeth twice a day, have "clean" breath, and use deodorants to hide their body smells.

Middle-class Americans have a more complex reaction to hair. A woman's beautiful hairdo is appreciated by all, but hair on her legs is not. Men generally are expected to have short hair on their heads and no hair on their faces. A mustache will be tolerated; a beard, however, causes a surprising amount of mistrust and resentment.

Finally, a word about weight. Professional people in America usually want to look slim; if they are not slim, they are expected to try to lose weight. The prejudice against fat, like that against hair, may strike the nonnative professional as extreme, but it cannot be ignored.

Dress. The standard of dress for men in many professions is a conservative (usually black, blue, or gray) suit, a tie, and a white or light-colored shirt. The tie should be dark, possibly solid in color, or with conservative stripes or patterns; it is to be kept tight around the neck, although it may be loosened after 5 p.m. or in very hot temperatures. Business professionals rarely remove their coats except at these times, or when working with people they know well. The "white collar/blue collar" distinction is very real even today: The man who works in an open-neck "blue" shirt and no coat does not seem professional to many Americans.

Professional women are expected to be attractive and somewhat less conservative than men in their dress; usually they avoid slacks, however, preferring suits with skirts. At the other extreme is overdressing: Unlike a man, who may wear the same suit to the office and to a party, a woman usually wears bright, tight, or revealing clothes only to the party—not to the office. Similarly, jewelry, loose hair, and pronounced makeup are suitable only on social occasions.

The Courtesies of Conversation

Conversation consists of language—or so we think. Actually, conversation is full of nonverbal communication. Often we make people like or dislike us, not by what we say, but by our behavior in talking to them.

Personal space has already been discussed. Three other nonverbal parts of conversation remain to be considered: introductions, body control, and eye contact.

Introductions. Let us assume that Mr. X and his sister, Ms. X, who are nonnative speakers of English, are invited to a reception for an American politician. At the reception they are introduced to Mr. and Mrs. Smith, an important businessman and his wife. Let us look at the introductions and then at several minutes of the conversation.

The men are introduced first, and they shake hands. Mr. X does not try to break Mr. Smith's hand, nor pump it. He squeezes it firmly for about one second, then releases it. At this point Mr. Smith presents Mr. X to his wife. Mr. X does not offer his hand, but Mrs. Smith extends hers, and he grasps it briefly and gently.

Now Mr. X presents his sister to Mr. and Mrs. Smith. Ms. X may or may not choose to give her hand to Mr. Smith; modern American women usually do. If she is older than Mrs. Smith, she has the same choice, but if Mrs. Smith is older, Ms. X should wait for Mrs. Smith to offer her hand. (The formal greeting is, of course, "How do you do?" Either "I'm happy to meet you" or "It's nice to meet you" is also polite.)

Body control. The four people form a circle to talk, so that each person can see every other person's face. Because Mr. X and Ms. X do not know the Smiths well yet, they stand very straight, like the people in Figure 1, shifting their weight from one foot to the other. Of course, they do not touch the Smiths. If Mr. Smith accidentally touches Mr. X's arm, he apologizes.

At this time all four people will likely clasp their hands together. The men may hold their hands behind them or in front of them; the women will clasp hands in front or hold a handbag. They make gestures occasionally as they speak and then fold their hands together again.

Now the two couples discover, however, that they like each other. Their bodies relax slightly. Mr. Smith folds his arms over his chest and smiles. Mrs. Smith touches Ms. X's arm very lightly. Ms. X and her brother smile in appreciation but, remembering English speakers' reserve, do not touch the Smiths in return. They *do* gesture as they speak, but gently. They also laugh, but softly.

Eye contact. Perhaps Mr. and Mrs. Smith like the two foreigners because of their eyes—or more accurately, because of their correct use of eye contact. Every culture has its rules for the way people should look at each other. One of the causes of racial tension in the United States, for example, is blacks' and whites' differing ideas of eye contact.

In the professional subculture, which includes middle-class blacks as well as whites, the rule calls for a steady but broken gaze into each other's eyes. Thus, when Mr. Smith talks, he shifts his gaze from Mr. X to Ms. X to Mrs. Smith, and they all look into his eyes; this is the way they prove they are listening to him (even if they are not). When Mr. X responds, he tries to make eye contact with all the others.

The two men and the two women then begin separate conversations. Mr. X looks steadily into Mr. Smith's eyes, but after every 3 or 4 seconds he looks away briefly; to "stare" is impolite. He does not look at the floor, for this means sullenness or lack of self-confidence. Nor does he stare at the ceiling or a wall; this would mean boredom. Mr. X also makes small sounds when Mr. Smith pauses, to show that he understands (even if he doesn't): "Um-hum," "I see," or "Ah yes" are said softly. These little noises are very necessary.

Mr. Smith now stops talking and looks over Mr. X's shoulder. This is a sign that he feels the conversation should end. Thus Mr. X, who obviously understands Mr. Smith's culture very well, suggests to his sister that they should "go for a drink." The Smiths are pleased and offer their hands again. As they move apart, Mrs. Smith may even say to her husband, "Ms. X and her brother are very nice. Perhaps we could invite them to dinner some time."

To conclude the story: A friendship has been formed, probably because of good manners (by American standards) rather than good conversation.

Establishing Good Working Relationships

Because the English-speaking cultures are democratic, everyone in the company is important to the working professional. A professional will not advance in the company simply by flattering the boss and ignoring the secretaries. A few words are therefore needed to suggest ways of winning approval in the workplace.

The boss. Although some supervisors do like flattery, almost all supervisors like the following qualities in the people who work for them: competence (the ability to do assigned tasks well); punctuality; a willingness to work overtime; a neat, attractive appearance; a positive attitude; and discretion (knowing when to talk and when to say nothing).

They will *not* appreciate a subservient attitude. A professional person who says "Yes sir" constantly, who stands far back, who keeps his or her eyes lowered, and who always speaks softly will probably not be promoted.

Peers. Normally, our closest relationships in the working situation are with peers (people at our own level). Peers may not be helpful in our attempts to advance in the organization, but they can offer the nonnative speaker something else: friendship.

A foreigner sometimes has difficulty being accepted into a group of native speakers, who understand each other better than they understand the "outsider." The nonnative speaker takes the first step toward gaining acceptance by always doing his or her share of the work, and by aiding the others when asked to do so. Cheerfulness also helps; so does polite conversation. If a colleague looks sick, it is proper to express concern; if a colleague's spouse has been sick, it is proper to ask if he or she is getting better.

Of course, friendship depends on shared interests—things to talk about. Foreign men usually need to know something about sports (especially football and baseball). Foreign women might show an interest in recipes and shopping centers. Probably, both men and women should know something about popular television shows. As poor as many shows are, they form the topic of much daily conversation (and they do give lessons in both American culture and English).

Among American men, the first sign that a foreigner has been accepted is a smile. The second sign is probably casual conversation—stopping to talk to the "newcomer." Then there are two very strong signals: touch—such as a slap on the back or a hand on the arm—and teasing, which indicates acceptance. Even if American men tease the nonnative speaker about his accent, they are usually being friendly, not cruel. (Women are less likely to tease; they may show acceptance of a foreign woman by confiding personal problems.)

There are also rituals which show acceptance. Usually these involve food and drink, as when two colleagues discuss a problem over a cup of coffee. The next step may be lunch together; nonnative speakers should always accept an invitation to a "business lunch" (although they pay for their own meals). Particularly among men, the third step—and a sign of affection—is an invitation to "have a drink" after work.

The final step is an invitation to dinner in the colleague's home. This is an offer of friendship, and nonnative speakers may make the offer before the American does. But they must be sure that the American is ready; the signals listed above should have been given first. Probably they should also express the invitation very generally the first time: "Maybe you would like to try our native cooking sometime—?" If the American hesitates, the invitation may have come too soon.

Subordinates. Secretaries, lab technicians, clerks, and foremen: All the people who work for professionals are important to them. A wise person will not ignore them, reject their suggestions, or treat them as inferiors. Subordinates will accept direction, but not dictatorship.

A special note must be made of secretaries. Like the professions, the position of secretary has time-honored traditions and standards. In America, secretaries, who are usually women, often deal directly with business clients and other professional people. Typically, they handle the complex arrangements which make meetings and other professional contacts possible.

In return, they expect respect. Professionals should listen to a secretary's advice, even if they don't follow it. They should show their appreciation with gifts on appropriate occasions, and with thanks for jobs well done. In brief, the secretary is an important person and should be treated like one.

Summary

In many social situations, nonverbal communication is as important as words. The nonnative speaker working in an English-speaking culture communicates effectively by adapting to local conventions regarding time, space, and grooming. Even conversational skills and good working relationships can be established in the absence of perfect English.

Chapter 3

Public Speaking

Professionally trained men and women must expect to give speeches occasionally, even if only short talks to people in their own organizations. To a nonnative speaker, giving a speech in English may seem a difficult assignment, but there is much more to public speaking than language.

In fact, many compensatory, nonlinguistic skills are important in preparing a speech. Among these are good organization, a mature, objective tone, and a special style of body language. Above all, the preparation of a speech means practice.

Because preparation is so important, we will spend several paragraphs on the process of getting ready. Thereafter, we will explore the nonverbal aspects of delivering the speech.

Preparation

Even short speeches need preparation. Our first experience, for example, may be the introduction of another speaker, and may last only a minute or two. Yet we must accomplish four goals:

1. Deliver an opening line to gain the audience's attention, and refer to the occasion which brought them together.
2. Discuss, accurately, the speaker's background and qualifications.
3. State the speaker's name, and the title of the speech, exactly.
4. Stimulate audience interest in the topic.

Even a 1-minute introduction may take an hour of preparation.

A long talk meant to persuade or inform the audience on a subject requires much more preparation. Let us assume that a foreign-born professional man is asked to give a 20-minute talk—in English of course, although his grammar and pronunciation are both flawed. He begins to prepare himself psychologically as well as intellectually.

18

Attitude.   Even native speakers, if they are inexperienced, do not like to speak to large groups. The first task of the person giving the speech, therefore, is to build self-confidence. He needs to tell himself, "I can do it, and I'm going to do it well."

Thinking positively about the audience also helps self-confidence. Audiences are usually friendly. If the speaker is also friendly, and prepared with a good talk, the audience will respond with smiles and applause. The speaker should try to feel warm and grateful toward them in advance.

Next he considers this question: What ideas will they want to hear? If he is wise, he will choose a topic that will be useful to them, as well as one that he enjoys discussing. In short, he chooses something in his professional area.

Already he should feel confident, and he must stay confident. Good speakers are those who appear to be enjoying their own speeches. Usually they *do* enjoy them, and so do their audiences.

Putting the speech together.   With his topic, or thesis, in mind, the speaker outlines his major ideas. The introduction and conclusion can be developed later. First he gets the body of the talk together, by arranging his points in a straight line—by chronology or by a series of causes, effects, or arguments. (For a discussion of effective organization, see Part III.) Everything he includes is relevant to his main point, or thesis.

Some speeches make very general points; they are usually meant to inspire. An informative speech by a professional person, however, requires detail to support the major statements. In writing, we tend to use facts and figures, and these may be used in a speech too. Statements by other experts also work very well in public speaking. It is often best to use examples, however, because the audience can remember examples more easily than statistics.

As an illustration, consider a management consultant (in this case, a woman) speaking to a group of executives about improving employee morale. She states the idea that praising an employee for performance in a specific situation has positive effects. Her point might be supported in several ways:

1. *Expert testimony.* "Dr. C. J. Smith, probably the leading researcher in the field, puts it this way: 'Although an employee may not know it, the supervisor's praise for a good job is more important in keeping him or her productive and satisfied than salary increases.'"

2. *Quantification.* "A recent study of supervisor traits and productivity at the X Corporation showed a .97 correlation between productivity and immediate, specific praise from the supervisor. The correlation was only

.57 for generalized praise or appreciation by the supervisor, which ranked below other factors such as accessibility and clear direction."

3. *Example.* "Someone once asked Bill Jones, President of Y Company, how he had moved to the top so quickly. He said that, in his first year there, when he was a production engineer, he had allowed a machine to overheat, and needed to make a quick decision. Should he take a chance on its cooling slowly, or shut down the operation, which would reveal his mistake? He decided to shut down. Later he discovered that the machine was defective; at the time, however, he feared his manager's reaction. The manager came out on the floor while he and his crew were shutting down. Jones admitted his mistake and expected criticism. Instead, his manager said, 'That was quick thinking. You made the right decision.' Jones claims that he has been trying to repay that compliment ever since."

Clearly, an example or story takes longer, and may not be "proof," but it is effective in public speaking, for the audience usually remembers it.

Thus, our speaker makes certain that his statements are documented by one means or another. He now has the body of his speech ready, and he can turn to the introduction and conclusion. The introduction should last no more than 2 minutes in a 20-minute speech. Perhaps he will tell the audience, with some humor, how he got interested in his subject. Or he could ask them if they have ever considered its importance. A good introduction would also include a summary of the points to be covered. Note that a speech must contain some repetition of ideas in any case, since a listener (unlike a reader) cannot turn back a page.

Similarly, the conclusion could contain a summary of the major points. On the other hand, an audience may not be satisfied with a summary. To make a good conclusion, the speaker should try to have a general statement which restates his main idea. This could be a quotation from a poet or a world figure, an amusing comment, or a rhetorical question. Since the last line may be the one the audience remembers best, it must be prepared carefully.

The speech is now drafted. At this point, two questions arise: Should the speaker write it all carefully and read it to the audience? Or should he memorize it? The answer to both questions is "no." Audiences are bored by read speeches, while a speaker who has memorized his talk may become confused if he forgets a word or a phrase. The voice rhythms are also wrong; speeches read or spoken from memory sound unnatural.

Rather, the speaker should place his thoughts into an extended outline and then put them on note cards. He writes out quotes, statistics, and his sources exactly, but reduces his own ideas to short headings that will fit on the cards. Each of these headings is simply a reminder to him. This way he will not get lost, but he can still talk naturally to his audience.

Next, with cards in hand, he practices the speech, looking at key words, and then raising his eyes to speak. Certain words may be difficult to pronounce; he says them several times. As new ideas come, he makes notes on the cards. He practices gestures which feel comfortable and looks into a mirror to see if they seem right. Finally, he times the speech, to find out if it will last approximately 20 minutes. An inexperienced speaker may be surprised: The talk may last only 10 minutes, or it may last 40 minutes. In either case, he must make revisions.

There are still a few steps to be taken in preparation for the speech. The note cards have to be rewritten for easy reading. The speaker should also try to anticipate questions the audience will ask after he has concluded. To be safe, he will practice the speech without notes; probably he will forget a few details, but he may think of something interesting to add. Or he may give the speech before a friend, to get his or her comments, or speak into a tape recorder and listen to himself.

If he has done all this, he will feel confident and will look forward to giving the speech.

Delivering the Speech

It is normal to be anxious on the day of the speech; often the speaker is simply impatient to start. The subjects to be discussed here are, first, how to start well, and second, how to communicate well *nonverbally* in giving the speech.

Getting started.   As the speaker waits to be introduced, he naturally thinks about his talk and rehearses it in his mind. Yet he must try to observe the events around him. Good speakers will make some connection between these events and their subjects, and actually revise their opening statements so that the beginning line is a natural transition to the talk.

All through the period before the speech begins, the speaker tries to appear calm and comfortable. The note cards should be kept out of sight—or at least, they should not be read. The speaker must be prepared to speak with other people near him, to listen to them, and to smile pleasantly.

Next, he must listen carefully to the introduction. Perhaps the person introducing him will say something he should respond to. Again, this may suggest a change in his opening line. At least, he must think of a way to thank the introducer and to show that he has listened.

When the introduction is complete, he rises and walks steadily to his place. (Those who are nervous can calm themselves by taking deep breaths.) In fact, he will try to walk just the way he would if he were answering a knock at the front door of his home.

Standing before the audience now, he does not begin his talk immediately. He must demonstrate his calm and relaxation. He might take a moment, therefore, to place his note cards on the podium and then to thank the person who has introduced him. It is a good idea to wait another few seconds, looking at the audience to be sure they are settled and ready to listen.

Delivery.   The speaker has not yet said a word to the audience. If his behavior has been cheerful and calm, however, they are already under control. What remains is to keep them under control, mainly through nonverbal communicative acts.

First, his eyes should move from face to face around the hall. He can't look at all of the people there but he can pretend that he is entering a private conversation with each of them. This is reassuring to an audience, but it also helps the speaker, who must know the listeners' reaction. If they smile or nod in agreement, he is doing well; if they frown or look bored, he is not, and must adjust.

Second, he must speak at a normal rate. If the speaker's pronunciation is not clear to an English-speaking audience, he must avoid speaking quickly; nonnative speakers should be careful, in particular, to pronounce consonants at the ends of words. Speeches will also fail if the audience cannot hear or if they feel the speaker is shouting at them. The speaker watches the audience to get their reaction; he may even ask, at the beginning, if everyone can hear.

Third, his body should seem relaxed. As he begins, he spreads his feet slightly, so that he does not look stiff. His hands can be placed on the podium, as long as he does not lean on it. An erect posture, with hands lightly clasping the sides of the podium, gives the appearance of relaxation.

Of course, the speaker cannot simply stand in one position throughout the speech. The audience's attention is not held by words alone, but by the speaker's movement as well. All good speakers gesture, for example, to support their points. They also turn their bodies to the left or right, step back, or even step out from behind the podium.

Even while he is speaking and moving about, our speaker continues to look at his audience, dropping his eyes only briefly to his notecards. Clearly, only thorough preparation enables him to carry out so many activities at once. Furthermore, only good preparation enables him to relax and to move freely. The well-prepared speaker *does* relax; indeed, he may find speaking a thrilling experience.

A final note for speaking effectively must be added here. The speaker must control not only his nervousness but his enthusiasm. The audience is really there to hear ideas, not to look at the person speaking. The speaker should stay with his planned talk, and also with his 20-minute limit.

At the end of his speech, he gives his conclusion as he rehearsed it, steps back, and nods. He should be prepared then for questions from the audience; usually the person who has introduced him will call on people who raise their hands, and that person will also cut off questions when it is time to end.

Summary

The hard work in giving a speech—for native as well as nonnative professionals—is not the speech itself. Rather, it is preparation, which builds the speaker's self-confidence and shapes his or her ideas into a logical pattern. Many experts believe that, indeed, the well-prepared speech is 90 percent given before the speaker begins. Once before the audience, the speaker's tasks are to keep the body loose, to use controlled gestures, to make eye contact, and to speak clearly while varying the pitch and volume of his or her voice.

Chapter 4

Oral Presentations

A major theme of this book is the idea that communication in the English-speaking professional world consists of much more than using English. We have seen that the nonnative professional can communicate well through a knowledge of cultural cues and body language, and can give a successful speech by organizing and rehearsing it carefully. To end this part, here is another practical guide to good oral communication which involves no words.

Our subject is the technical presentation, or demonstration. A presentation is like a speech, except that the purpose of the speaker is to explain a technical point or perhaps even "sell" the audience on a project or device. This audience may contain the speaker's supervisor or an important client, who urgently needs the information being presented, and wants it to be communicated as quickly and as accurately as possible.

In this situation, the presenter needs the help of audiovisual aids. Below is a review of the aids at a speaker's disposal and ways to use them effectively. This review is followed by a general discussion of preparation for the presentation.

Audiovisual Aids

Modern technology has supplied professionals with a great variety of machines as vehicles for information in oral presentations. It is also true that the presenters themselves must prepare the information and feed it to the machines. Consequently, the aids, or media, described below are the simplest to use and generally do not require the assistance of an expert.

Three-dimensional aids. The architect's model, the engineer's "mock-up," and the geographer's physical map are all examples of visuals which are usually created by the professional's own hands; in many cases they will be more useful, and more satisfying to the audience, than two-dimensional images. The major requirements for three-dimensional aids are that they should be large enough for the audience to see, reasonably accurate, and—above all—attractive.

Easel graphics.   Upright surfaces for showing visual information are also useful, non-electronic aids; in addition, they are simpler to prepare. The most common of these "easel graphics" are the chalkboard, the felt board, and the flip chart.

The chalkboard is used more often in schools and universities than in the business office. Despite new types of surfaces, and new types of "chalk," writing (and erasing) on chalkboards remains a rather dirty process. It also requires turning away from the audience. Finally, it may suggest a teacher–student relationship between presenter and audience, which English-speaking professionals may not appreciate.

Felt boards are more neutral, and cleaner, but they require much advance preparation. Their name comes from the material—felt, or flannel—used as a surface, on which prepared, felt-backed signs will stick. Since the visual must be large enough for the audience to see, very few signs can be mounted at one time. Furthermore, they may fall off; similarly, presenters may distract themselves and their audiences as they put signs on, straighten them, remove them, and so on.

Both chalkboards and felt boards, therefore, have disadvantages. The flip chart (Figure 2) seems more efficient. It consists of an easel holding a pad of large sheets of heavy paper, which can be "flipped" over the top of the easel to show the next sheet. Of course, the visuals on the sheets

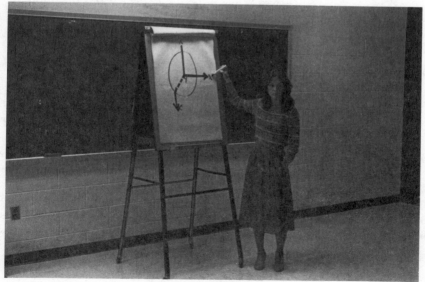

FIG. 2. *Flip chart.*

should be prepared in advance, but they can be revised during the presentation. The flipping activity also tends to be less distracting than the activity of hanging and removing signs.

A final note: Easel graphics are appropriate for small audiences—usually, fewer than 75 people. Electronic media are needed for large audiences.

Reproducing machines.   The presenter needs to distinguish between two sorts of visual information: that which the listeners should notice, to help them understand; and that which they should review, to help them remember. Important printed materials, either visual or verbal, should be reproduced in bulk and distributed to the audience. Certainly the audience does not need the entire text of the presentation; rather, they might be given two to four pages of major points or key visuals.

The quality of the reproduced materials should be professional—that is, well organized in content and neat in appearance. Materials which are difficult to read will influence an audience unfavorably toward the presentation. Probably the presenter should avoid reproduction on mimeograph or ditto machines, which now seem primitive. The standard practice is to type materials and photocopy them; the type must be dark and the copies "clean" (that is, without specks, shadows, or carbon smears). A very impressive—but expensive—method is to have the materials professionally printed.

The method of distributing the materials must also be considered. They should not be handed out during the presentation, because the audience's attention will be distracted. Rather, the presenter asks the listeners to pick up their copies as they come in the door, if he or she wants them to refer to the copies during the presentation. On the other hand, if the audience needs to listen and watch carefully, and *not* read, the presenter should ask them to take copies on their way out.

Overhead projectors.   An extremely useful device for displaying visuals during the presentation is the overhead projector (Figure 3), which throws light through a transparent piece of acetate and onto a screen. The presenter draws the visual on the acetate before the talk, sets it on top of the projector, and flips a switch when it is to be shown. He or she does not have to stand behind the machine, back to the audience, but continues to face them. The lights in the room may be kept on or turned off; the projector throws off enough light for the presenter to read notes.

The overhead projector has a further benefit: It allows the presenter to alter the visual, or to add details. First, he or she may draw in changes (with a grease pen) while the audience watches. Or the presenter may place a second transparency on top of the first, so that both are shown.

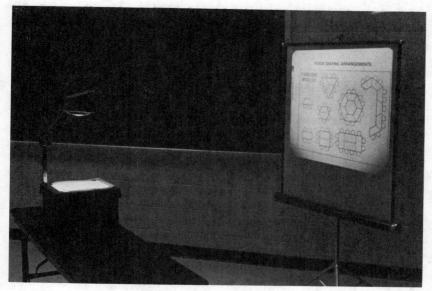

FIG. 3. *Overhead projector.*

The overhead projector has all the advantages of a flip chart, and more. It is easier to carry, it is mechanically as simple, and it can be used with a larger audience (100 to 200 people).

Slide projectors.   Projecting visuals clearly to large audiences usually requires complex equipment, such as slide or film projectors. These force the presenter to work in a darkened room. Often they require the help of expert technicians, both in production and in projection, and the entire process can be very expensive.

It is true, however, that slide projectors are widely used, particularly at scientific meetings. Slides effectively show color; they also have a sharper focus than overhead transparencies. A further advantage is that an oral presentation may be recorded in advance and timed to accompany the slides. Obviously, when a presentation is to be given more than once, the presenter should consider preparing it this way.

Videotape machines.   A newer medium, which offers great possibilities to the individual presenter, is the videotape projector. In the past, videotape could not be projected clearly across a large room. The tape had to be played into a television monitor, and therefore it could not be seen by a large audience, unless many monitors were used.

Videotape technology is developing very rapidly, however. Lightweight, comparatively inexpensive videotape recorders are available which both record an event and play it back; the tape can be erased and re-used, and projection is possible. Newer machines record both sound and image on a disc—much like a music record for a stereo set—and produce sharp pictures. Operating costs for either tapes or discs are low compared with the expense of using film.

Experts predict that videotaping will play a great role in professional presentations of the future. A reference work on its use is listed under "Further Reading" at the end of this first part of the book.

Preparation

When Thomas Edison was asked to explain how he made so many brilliant inventions, he replied: "Genius is one percent inspiration and ninety-nine percent perspiration." The same proportions apply to performance and preparation in the oral presentation. Success or failure usually depends on the amount of "sweat" that goes into getting ready.

In the following paragraphs, several questions are raised which every effective presenter must be able to answer.

Audience.   Presenters must know who is coming to hear the talk, and be able to put themselves in the listeners' place. What does the audience want to know? Will they be able to understand a very technical explanation? What questions will they ask?

Media.   Both the size of the audience and the nature of the message will determine what media should be used. (Usually, a presenter chooses only one or two aids.) Should any visuals or major statements be reproduced and distributed? What is the correct balance between words and visuals? Should the presenter draw his or her own visuals or seek expert assistance?

Setting.   Careful presenters assume nothing: They inspect the room and all arrangements. Is the room big enough (or small enough)? Is it quiet? Can light be shut out so that a projector can be used? Where should the flip chart or overhead projector be set? Are there outlets in the right places for electronic media? Is there a screen at the front of the room, and is it mechanically in order?

These questions should be settled a week ahead of time. But on the day of the presentation, the presenter makes a final check. Are the media in the right place, plugged in, and in working order? Is the room warm (or cool) enough? Is there a convenient table for the reproduced materials? Is the first visual on the flip chart visible, or covered, as it should be? Are the transparencies for the overhead projector stacked in the right order? If a three-dimensional model has been prepared, is it sitting where everyone can see it? And so on.

The rule is the same whether we are talking about preparation of the talk itself (Chapter 3) or preparation of the aids and the setting: Leave nothing to chance.

Summary

An oral presentation using audiovisual aids is a common fact of the professional's career. As in writing, visual materials complement, and simplify, the presenter's talk. The media used to show the materials are chosen to suit the audience and the message, and should be limited to one or two types. Ultimately, it is good preparation of the entire presentation which will bring success.

Further Reading

Hall, Edward T. *Beyond Culture*. New York: Anchor Press, 1976

Hall, Edward T. *The Hidden Dimension*. New York: Anchor Press, 1969

Hall, Edward T. *The Silent Language*. Greenwich, Conn.: Fawcett Publications, 1959

Mattingly, Grayson, and Welby Smith. *Introducing the Single-Camera VTR System: A Layman's Guide to Video-Recording*. New York: Scribners, 1973

Molloy, John. *Dress for Success*. New York: P. H. Wyden, 1975

Molloy, John. *The Woman's Dress for Success Book*. New York: Warner Books, 1978

Monroe, Alan H., and Douglas Ehringer. *Principles of Speech Communication*. Glenview, Ill.: Scott, Foresman, 1975

Parsons, Edgar. *Audio-Visual Communications for Associations*. Washington: Chamber of Commerce of the United States, 1974

Price, Stephen S. "Put Your Best Voice Forward." *Reader's Digest*, vol. 90, no. 539 (March, 1967), pp. 133–35

Rowe, Mack R., David Curl, Harvey R. Frye, Jerold Kemp, and Wilfred Veenendal. *The Message Is You: Guidelines for Preparing Presentations*. Washington: Association for Educational Communications and Technology, 1971

Samovar, Larry A., and Jack Mills. *Oral Communication: Message and Response*. Dubuque, Ia.: William C. Brown Co., 1972

Spradley, James P., and Michael A. Rynkiewich, eds. *The Nacirema: Readings on American Culture*. Boston: Little, Brown and Co., 1975

Timm, Paul R. *Managerial Communication: A Finger on the Pulse*. Englewood Cliffs, N.J.: Prentice-Hall, 1980

PART II

READING EFFECTIVELY IN ENGLISH

OBJECTIVES

- To summarize the major points of reading theory
- To suggest an active approach to reading
- To identify discourse markers and other signals
- To introduce summarization and other reductive modes of writing

Reading often, and reading well, is essential for all professional people, and especially for those who must write often. For nonnative speakers of English, reading English prose is a way of getting the "feel" of the language—and, incidentally, the feel of English spelling. It is widely believed that good writing in fact depends upon effective reading.

Professionals must, of course, read well if they are to understand new developments in their fields. The two purposes—reading for content and reading for control of the language—are mostly accomplished through the same training. Reading specialists have developed several "do's" and "don't's" for readers, which are summarized in Chapter 5. These rules apply to general reading materials, less so to highly technical materials.

In Chapters 6 to 8, processes are suggested for effective comprehension and retention of a general reading passage. These include identifying the writer's signals, marking important points in a text, and reducing the writer's ideas to their basic core.

Chapter 5

Practical Applications of Reading Theory

Reading ability does not depend entirely on language. Nonnative speakers of English will read English better if they are good readers in their own languages. Similarly, both nonnative and native speakers of English who read poorly are probably making the same mistakes.

It is worthwhile, then, to look briefly at the theories developed by reading specialists. First, the causes of poor reading are reviewed, and then the possible solutions for nonnative speakers are considered. The final section of this chapter discusses the problem of retaining what has been learned.

Slow Reading

Often, people read slowly in the belief that they will understand better. Except with highly technical materials, the reverse seems to be true: Slow readers tend to comprehend less—and forget more. Specialists associate effective reading with the ability to read quickly.

Thus, the principal problems in reading effectively are the habits which cause us to read slowly. They are summarized below.

Mouthing the words.   Reading aloud, or simply mouthing the words, convinces some readers that they are ignoring nothing and understanding everything. Yet we can read a totally unfamiliar language aloud while comprehending, of course, nothing. Moreover, it is almost impossible to mouth words at a faster rate than 150 to 175 words per minute. This is considered a slow reading rate.

Regressing.   Some readers make a habit of looking back a line or two and reading again. This process is called backtracking, or regressing. Naturally, it slows the overall reading rate. It should not be confused with re-reading carefully, or reviewing, a passage which has already been completed. Rather, regressing is the habit of stopping, sometimes in mid-sentence, and starting again. It interrupts the natural flow of learning from the printed page.

Slow eye movement.   Our eyes are often lazy. They may not want to see more than one word at a time or to move quickly. Reading quickly— which, again, is reading effectively—requires the reader to see a group of words simultaneously, and to shift the eyes quickly to the next group. To make the eyes work, the brain must work, and the reader therefore understands better.

Poor vocabulary.   When readers encounter a new word, their tendency is to stop, to look at it, and perhaps to put their books down so that they may search in the dictionary. While looking up the word, however, they lose the general idea of the material being read. The nonnative speaker finds it both natural and necessary to make such stops, but ineffective reading results.

Failure to note signals.   Good writing is full of signals to the reader— signals such as headings or topic sentences which lead from one main idea to another. It is these main ideas which the good reader sees and comprehends. The poor reader often treats all words and sentences equally; he or she sees all the details but is slowed by them, and often does not comprehend the main ideas.

Adaptation of Reading Theory to the Nonnative Speaker

Poor reading in English may derive from one or more of the bad habits described above. Nonnative speakers can stop some of these bad habits through practice. Regressing is an example. No instructor is needed to keep the reader moving forward; indeed, readers must be their own instructors.

Slow eye movement may be a more difficult habit to break, but again, it is not entirely a language problem. English learners who read only a word at a time in English probably read the same way in their own languages. They will shift their eyes 8 to 12 times for a single line of print in a book, and may spend one-half second on each shift. The good reader makes half as many shifts, more than *twice* as quickly.

Nonnative speakers who can read this book are capable of reading English words in clusters. If they do not, they can and should train themselves to do so and should attempt to shift their eyes more quickly.

Now we look at poor habits which raise special questions for nonnative speakers.

Reading aloud.   Nonnative speakers are often advised to read aloud. The practice is most useful, however, for those who have not yet mastered the sounds of English words and the syntax of English sentences. Advanced learners are advised to read silently.

Learning vocabulary.   The most obvious handicap of nonnative speakers is their limited vocabulary. Nevertheless, it is recommended that they *not* stop immediately to look up a word they do not understand. Rather, they should try to guess the meaning from context, or perhaps from its Latin or Greek origins. Only when they have finished the chapter, the section, or at least the paragraph should they consult the dictionary, and then only if they have not guessed the word's meaning from context.

Further steps are necessary if the new word is to be remembered. Unfortunately, we usually forget definitions. The new word should be written down, with its definition, and then used several times so that it becomes part of the learner's active vocabulary. One further recommendation: An English dictionary, not a bilingual dictionary, should be used.

Learning the signals.   The signals a writer gives to a reader include headings, topic sentences, and transition words. These are not necessarily a language problem for the nonnative speaker, but they may be a cultural problem: They are a custom in the "culture" of good English writers. As such, they can be learned cognitively and will be discussed later (see Chapter 6).

First, we shall look more closely at the purpose of effective reading, which is effective learning.

Retention

The words "comprehending" and "understanding" have been used often in the previous pages. Understanding is not enough for professional people, however. To be truly effective readers, we must retain the knowledge that has been gained from reading. We must understand something before we can retain or know it, but we may lose it after we have understood it.

Figure 4 demonstrates the problem. The first point to notice is that we normally forget 80 percent of a reading passage within 2 weeks. On the other hand, if we review the passage immediately after we have read it, we will retain most of the information learned.

Reading specialists suggest other steps toward increased comprehension and retention. These steps are summarized below (and will be developed in Chapters 6, 7, and 8).

Prereading.   We often find what we are actively looking for. We should ask ourselves why we are reading an article and what we expect

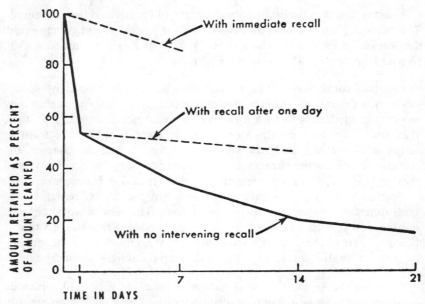

FIG. 4. *Reading retention. [Figure 1 (p. 4) from Effective Reading by Francis P. Robinson. Copyright © 1962 by Francis P. Robinson. Reprinted by permission of Harper & Row, Publishers, Inc.]*

to find in it. This process is aided by a quick review of the article, called "skimming."

Skimming an article means looking through it rapidly for the main ideas, which are found in the title, the headings, topic sentences in the paragraphs, special connecting terms, stressed words, and the conclusion. With a feeling for the important points, we then generate a series of questions which we expect the article to answer. The brain has now been put into action; we are ready to engage the author in a dialogue.

Active reading.   In reading the article, we try to read quickly, avoiding the errors mentioned at the beginning of this chapter. We also attempt to grasp all the important ideas, in two ways: First, we look for answers to the questions we raised; second, we mark the main ideas or make quick notes about them.

As discussed earlier, the reader should not stop until at least a paragraph, or preferably a section, has been read. It is therefore inappropriate to stop often and write, in longhand, extensive notes on the major ideas. One permissible practice is to make marginalia—to write notes, in the reader's own words, in the margins. Brief notes on a separate sheet of paper are also acceptable.

An alternative method—marking important ideas—is suggested in Chapter 7. Whatever method is used, it must not break the flow of ideas in the passage being read. Nonnative speakers should read until their concentration begins to fail, make a quick note, and read on.

They should *not* expect to understand everything. Nonnative speakers who set a goal of perfect comprehension often become nervous about reading—and thus read less effectively. Reading well in a second language requires relaxation, just as speaking does.

Reciting.   When the article has been read, we should "recite" our knowledge. First, we try to answer the questions we developed at the beginning. We cover our marginalia or notes and work from memory. Whenever we cannot remember the main points, we reexamine them. It is then appropriate to write notes at more length, from memory and in our own words. Exact quotations are not helpful, particularly not for nonnative speakers.

As Figure 4 indicates, immediate recitation is the most efficient method for retaining information. Reviewing notes a day or two later is also helpful, however, as a test of comprehension and retention. Finally, discussing the article with colleagues is a valuable, active form of recitation.

Summary

According to reading specialists, readers must discipline themselves to move their eyes quickly. They should also guess at the meanings of unknown words and stop only at the end of a long passage (preferably several paragraphs) to write notes. By adding prereading and recitation processes to the actual reading, they will retain what they have learned.

Chapter 6

Writers' Signals

Prereading, as stated in the preceding chapter, begins with skimming an article for its major points. It was further stated that the good writer of English plants signals to the reader, including the title, the headings, and the conclusion. These are easy to see, however. Two less obvious cues are discussed below: topic sentences and transition signals.

The model texts which will be analyzed in this chapter (and elsewhere in the rest of this part) come from a well-known book on social economics, *The Affluent Society*, by John Kenneth Galbraith (Boston: Houghton Mifflin, © 1958, 1969 by John Kenneth Galbraith. Reprinted by permission of Houghton Mifflin Company). The style is more graceful than that found in the usual technical composition, the paragraphs are sometimes long, and Galbraith's vocabulary is large. His ideas are always interesting, however; more importantly, he gives readers the signals they need.

Topic Sentences

It was pointed out above that readers should not concentrate on individual words. In fact, they should not slow down to study sentences. In good written English, the *paragraph* is the basic unit of discourse and is the smallest unit the reader should study.

Writers of English have a common understanding of the paragraph: It is a group of sentences which contains a main idea plus details that support or extend the main idea. One sentence is usually devoted to the main idea, or topic, and it is called the topic sentence. Here is a passage from *The Affluent Society* with topic sentences italicized.

II

Men fight for what is important to them, and the businessman who senses his self-interest will battle vigorously for a value system which

38

emphasizes the importance of production. Indeed, and perhaps more intuitively than otherwise, he already does. The business liturgy now accords an important place to resonant assertions of the vital role of production. "Only the productive can be strong. Only the strong can be free." "Production made America . . ." "Let us stop bickering and produce."

The widespread suspicion and even hostility of businessmen to government, even when, as in the case of the Eisenhower Administration, it was presumptively sympathetic to business, is one of the great constants in our political life. In part this is because the businessman is a sizable taxpayer and hence regards government services as in conflict with his economic interest. But . . . modern government also represents perhaps the major threat to the businessman's prestige. To the extent that problems of military defense, foreign policy, agricultural administration, public works, education, and social welfare are central to our thoughts, so the generals, foreign service officers, administrators, teachers, and other professional public servants are the popular heroes. Businessmen have almost certainly sensed this competition in modern times, and it is equally certain that it has conditioned their attitudes toward government. One of its manifestations is a vehement insistence that the government does not produce anything, that it is a barren whore. . . . The case involves some rather strained argument—it makes education unproductive and the manufacturer of the school toilet seats productive—but, nonetheless, it has a position of considerable prominence in the business liturgy.

A tension, perhaps ultimately more important, has also long existed between businessmen and the intellectuals. . . . As in the case of the government the basis of the tension has long been assumed to be economic. "The men whose research has given rise to new methods of production hate the businessmen who are merely interested in the cash value of their research work. It is very significant that such a large number of American research physicists sympathize with socialism and communism. . . . "* However, although the actual or suspected social radicalism of intellectuals may well contribute to hostility between businessmen and intellectuals, it is most doubtful if the tension would disappear even were intellectuals to conform their social attitudes to a line laid down by [a conservative senator]. Scientists, writers, professors, artists are also important competitors of the businessmen for public esteem.

This competition is especially noticeable in comment on public affairs—economic policy, foreign policy, the effect of government measures on popular morals and behavior. Perhaps the most honorific function in our time is that of social prophecy. No one enjoys quite such distinction as the man who, by common consent, is allowed to look ahead into the unknown and tell us what will happen and advise

---

* Ludwig von Mises, *The Anti-Capitalistic Mentality* (Princeton: Van Nostrand, 1956), p. 20.

us as to what we should do to promote or retard a particular occurrence. The intellectual naturally assumes his authority on these matters. He is likely to be gifted well beyond the businessman in erudition and oral capacity. That felicity the businessman counters by stressing his identification with production. He is not a "theorist" but a practical man. . . . Nothing is more suggestive in our social attitudes than the notion that almost any issue, however cosmic, can be best appreciated by a man who has had some practical experience with a lathe. Were anything to happen to the prestige of production, it is plain that the businessman, whose mystique is his identification with production, would suffer severely in his competition with the intellectual for the role of social prophet. If he wishes to defend himself in his present role, he must defend the importance of production. He can almost certainly be expected to do so.

There will be occasion presently for a further word on the competition between the businessman and the intellectual for contemporary esteem.

III

Politics have long been known to make incongruous bedfellows. More rarely, however, have those between the same sheets remained largely unaware of their intimate if odd companionship. This is the strange case with the vested interests in production. *Supporting the businessman on the all-importance of the production of goods is the professional American liberal.* The prestige which the businessman derives from production is reinforced by the nearly full weight of American liberal and radical comment. The reason for this alliance, though it requires some explanation, is not essentially complex. Men who hold tenaciously to a life raft may expect to be cast upon strange shores among strange companions. So it is with those who hold long enough to an idea amid changing currents and tides. . . . (*The Affluent Society*, pp. 183–187)

Model paragraphs.   In the section headed "II," Galbraith's paragraphs follow the classic model. One or two of them—particularly the one beginning "This competition . . ."—perhaps should be divided (and they have not been recopied entirely here, because of their length). Nevertheless each, excluding the last, begins with a general statement of the topic to be discussed, and the remainder of each paragraph supports the general statement.

The second paragraph may be taken as an example. The topic is the American businessman's hostility to government. Galbraith first suggests two causes for this hostility: (1) Businessmen see the government as an economic threat; and (2) more importantly, they see public officials as having more prestige than they themselves do. The remainder of the paragraph tells us how businessmen show their unhappiness.

Here also, the two parts of the paragraph could have suggested a division into two paragraphs. Nevertheless, all of the details in the paragraph fit with the topic sentence. When Galbraith moves to a new paragraph, it is to introduce a new topic: the tension between businessmen and intellectuals.

Exceptions.   At the end of section II, there is an exception. The last paragraph has only one sentence; it contains no "main idea" or "supporting details." The explanation is that it is a conclusion—but not a conclusion which summarizes major points. In this case, the conclusion is simply a signal to the reader that the discussion has ended.

Conclusions often do not follow the model. Other exceptions to the model are paragraphs of introduction or transition, which *announce* new ideas rather than *present* them. Moreover, there are many paragraphs in which the topic sentence does not appear at the beginning.

In the final paragraph of the passage quoted, the topic does not arrive until the fourth sentence. Sentence 1 is the restatement of an American proverb; it comments on the topic but does not identify it. Sentence 2 takes us a step closer to the topic and makes another comment, yet we still do not know who the "bedfellows" are. In sentence 3, we learn that the bedfellows are "vested interests," but they are still not identified. Finally, in sentence 4, the main idea is stated.

There are several reasons for a topic sentence appearing late in the paragraph (sometimes at the very end). Two important reasons are (1) to introduce a new topic without rushing into it, and (2) to build the reader's interest. Galbraith clearly has both reasons in mind. He is beginning a new section (III), and he is urging us to consider the irony of the alliance between liberals and businessmen.

Some searching, therefore, may be required to find a topic sentence. Occasionally, the main idea will be spread into two sentences, or if the writer is unskilled, there may be no topic sentence. In all cases it is proper to read the entire paragraph before identifying the main idea.

Discourse Markers

We turn now to a special group of function words called discourse markers—terms such as "therefore" or "by comparison" or "on the other hand." These markers, or signals, show the relationships between sentences and between paragraphs.

Galbraith is careful to plant discourse markers, just as he is careful to use topic sentences. Below, section III continues. A few paragraphs have been omitted; in them, he speaks of the American government's decision, in the 1930's, to stimulate production. The passage quoted is a discussion of the results, with discourse markers italicized.

> The rewards from a successful operation on the level of output were breathtaking. To increase production was to ameliorate unemployment, agricultural insecurity, the threat of bankruptcy to the small businessman, the risks of investors, the financial troubles of the states and cities, even the wretched overcrowding which results when people cannot afford to own or rent their own homes and must double up. Scarcely a single social problem was left untouched. And within a few years after Keynes the level of production became the critical factor in war mobilization. It was principally by increased output . . . that we provided for the war.
>
> *As a result*, production did more than impress the liberal. It became his program, and it established something akin to a monopoly over his mind. Here was perhaps the nearest thing to alchemy that had ever been seen in the field of politics. Increased production solved, or seemed to solve, nearly all of the social problems of the day.
>
> *Furthermore*, at least for a time, the practical concern for the total output of the economy was a liberal franchise. Conservatives hesitated to abandon the balanced budget, for so long a canon of the conventional wisdom. To do so was essential. To manipulate the level of production also meant that the role of government must be enlarged. This too was unpalatable to conservatives, for it accorded a prestige to government which had previously been accorded exclusively to private production.
>
> *Most important of all* for its influence on the liberal mind, the promise to raise production and reduce unemployment won elections. From the late thirties to the early fifties the promise to maintain high production and therewith high employment was the liberal's major claim to votes in the United States, and it was unbeatable. Very nearly the same thing was true of the left in Britain. (*The Affluent Society*, pp. 188–190)

Galbraith wants to show several effects of increased production on liberal thought. He begins with "As a result"—the clearest possible signal that his discourse is moving from cause to effect. His next paragraph adds another result; he therefore begins it with the additive marker, "furthermore." Because his third result is the most important, he begins the next paragraph with a signal which both adds and emphasizes: "Most important of all."

Not every paragraph will begin with discourse markers. Sometimes headings—even Roman numerals such as Galbraith uses—show the start of new ideas, and at other times transitions will be made by other means. The learner of English must be able to recognize discourse markers and their meanings, however. Like topic sentences, they are a quick guide to the content of a reading passage.

TABLE 1. *Types of discourse markers**

Notional Category/Meaning	Marker
1. *Enumerative.* Introduce the order in which points are to be made or the time sequence in which actions or processes took place.	first(ly), second(ly), third(ly), one, two three / a, b, c, next, then, finally, last(ly), in the first / second place, for one thing / for another thing, to begin with, subsequently, eventually, finally, in the end, to conclude.
2. *Additive*	
2.1 Reinforcing. Introduces a reinforcement or confirmation of what has preceded.	again, then again, also, moreover, furthermore, in addition, above all, what is more.
2.2 Similarity. Introduces a statement of similarity with what has preceded.	equally, likewise, similarly, correspondingly, in the same way.
2.3 Transition. Introduces a new stage in the sequence of presentation of information.	now, well, incidentally, by the way, O.K., fine.
3. *Logical Sequence*	
3.1 Summative. Introduces a summary of what has preceded.	so, so far, altogether, overall, then, thus, therefore, in short, to sum up, to conclude, to summarize.
3.2 Resultative. Introduces an expression of the result or consequence of what preceded (and includes inductive and deductive acts).	so, as a result, consequently, hence, now, therefore, thus, as a consequence, in consequence.
4. *Explicative.* Introduces an explanation or reformulation of what preceded.	namely, in other words, that is to say, better, rather, by (this) we mean.
5. *Illustrative.* Introduces an illustration or example of what preceded.	for example, for instance..
6. *Contrastive*	
6.1 Replacive. Introduces an alternative to what preceded.	alternatively, (or) again, (or) rather, (but) then, on the other hand.
6.2 Antithetic. Introduces information in opposition to what preceded.	conversely, instead, then, on the contrary, by contrast, on the other hand.
6.3 Concessive. Introduces information which is unexpected in view of what preceded.	anyway, anyhow, however, nevertheless, nonetheless, notwithstanding, still, though, yet, for all that, in spite of (that), at the same time, all the same.

* From Ronald Mackay, "Teaching the Information-Gathering Skills," in Mackay et al. (ed.), *Reading in a Second Language* (Rowley, Mass.: Newbury House, 1979), p. 88. Reprinted by permission of Newbury House Publishers, Inc., Rowley, MA.

As an aid to the learner, Table 1 lists the major discourse markers by function. There may be slight differences in meaning between some which perform the same function. Both *also* and *furthermore*, for example, show addition, but *furthermore* gives the new idea more emphasis. Learners of English should confirm their understanding of such words through practice and through reference to a dictionary.

Summary

In the prereading step of skimming, the learner needs to look at more than the title, headings, and conclusion. Discourse markers can be picked out rather easily, and are a guide to the flow of logic in the reading passage. Learners should also train themselves to find the topic sentence after they have finished a paragraph.

Chapter 7

Active Reading

Reading with a pen or pencil in hand can help us to understand an article. If our eyes do not always make our brains work, our hands usually will. At the same time, our hands must not take our attention away from the written materials.

Here is a paradox: The suggestion is that we respond in written words or symbols while reading—but do not stop reading. The only way to meet these contradictory goals is to use a personal "shorthand," or highly abbreviated response. One such response is marginalia; this approach is demonstrated briefly below. Thereafter, a method for marking a reading passage is suggested.

Marginalia

Writing in margins has several disadvantages. It is messy; it is hard on the paper; and when we review the passage, it could distract us from the author's own words. Beyond these problems, *lengthy* marginal notes take attention away from the author's ideas for too long a time.

Marginalia should therefore be short—and in English. Little more needs to be said about them, but two models follow. The first contains a paragraph from Galbraith which has already been quoted:

> As a result, production did more than impress the liberal. It became his program, and it established something akin to a monopoly over his mind. Here was perhaps the nearest thing to alchemy that had ever been seen in the field of politics. Increased production solved, or seemed to solve, nearly all of the social problems of the day.

Libl: Prod. solution to social problems

A marginal note for a short paragraph should be no longer than this one.

The second model is based on a passage from *The Closing Circle: Nature, Man and Technology*, by Barry Commoner. (Copyright © 1971 by Barry Commoner. Reprinted by permission of Alfred A. Knopf, Inc.) Commoner often writes on scientific matters for a popular audience. Here he discusses the loss of oxygen in Lake Erie.

Thus by the 1960's the western and central portions of the lake had switched from a well-oxygenated biological system to an oxygen-poor one. Important fish food had disappeared and fish that sought the cool bottom waters in the summer could not survive there for lack of oxygen. Only in the eastern basin, which is so deep that the water mass contains sufficient oxygen near its bottom even in the summer period of thermal stratification, were fish able to find cool waters well saturated with oxygen throughout the year. . . . What are the possible causes of such oxygen deficits?

[margin note: 1960's: Sudden loss of oxygen]

For a long time biologists have known about the oxygen demand created by the bacterial decay of organic wastes. A practical expression of this knowledge is the modern sewage treatment plant. . . . Sewage treatment involves a primary step in which indigestible solids are removed. This is followed by secondary treatment in a tank or pond rich in microbial decay organisms and usually artificially supplied with oxygen. Here, the organic materials that make up the bulk of sewage wastes are converted by microbial oxidation to inorganic substances. If the system works well, the resulting water is a clear dilute solution of the inorganic products of sewage treatment, of which nitrate and phosphate are most important. The waste's demand for oxygen is held within the secondary treatment pond where it can be met by an artificial air supply. The inorganic products of sewage treatment, which are free of BOD [biological oxygen demand], can then be released to rivers and lakes without causing an immediate drain on the oxygen available in the natural waters. . . .

[margin note: organic wastes consume oxygen; treatment should convert to inorganic]

The total mass of organic waste that reaches Lake Erie each year requires, for its conversion to inorganic salts, the consumption of about 180 million pounds of oxygen. A possible explanation of the recent oxygen deficits in the lake is the withdrawal of oxygen from lake water by the action of bacteria on this organic material. . . . It was found [in 1964] that the oxygen deficit in the bottom waters of the central basin alone was 270 million pounds of oxygen. This deficit developed over a period of only several weeks in only a part of the total mass of lake water, and must have been partially mitigated by oxygen entering the lake water. This means that Lake Erie, as a whole, must receive annually sufficient oxygen-demanding material to require the consumption of very considerably more than 270 million pounds of oxygen. If the organic wastes reaching the lake in a year can account for the consumption of only 180 million pounds of oxygen, somewhere in the lake there must be a very much larger oxygen demand, which is the main cause of the dangerously low levels of oxygen in lake water in recent summers. The key to the Lake Erie problem lies in discovering the nature and location of this huge, hidden source of oxygen demand.

Annual organic wastes poured in don't account for huge oxygen deficit.

In seeking for it, we need to recall that an effective primary and secondary sewage treatment plant will convert nearly all (about 90 per cent) of the organic matter originally present in the raw sewage into inorganic products. In this way, nearly all of the oxygen-consuming organic wastes in sewage are converted to nitrate and phosphate and discharged to surface waters which carry them out to sea.

Treatment should conv. org. matter to nit. + phos. to be carried out to sea.

It is now clear that this aim is being frustrated in Lake Erie, as it is in a growing number of the nation's water systems. Most of the inorganic products released into the lake as a result of waste treatment do *not* flow out of Lake Erie into the sea, but are reconverted into organic matter, much of which remains in the lake, where it makes the huge demand for oxygen that has been so disastrous for the lake's biology. (*The Closing Circle*, pp. 101–103)

Nit., phos. not carried out – reconv. to organic waste.

It can be seen that notes are not always efficient. The short fourth paragraph is not easily summarized; we need to read and understand the *fifth* paragraph in order to see the importance of the words " . . . surface waters which carry them out to sea." Again the lesson is that we should read as far as possible before stopping to make notes.

Marking the Text

In technical passages, marginalia may be impractical. Here is Commoner, for example, writing about increases in pollutants. Note the marks (including underlining) made on the text:

A good example of this trend is provided by <u>phosphate</u>, an important pollutant of surface waters. In the thirty-year period from

1910 to 1940 annual phosphate output from municipal sewage somewhat more than doubled, from about 17 million pounds (calculated as phosphorus) to about 40 million pounds. Thereafter the rate of phosphate output rose rapidly, so that in the next thirty-year period, 1940 to 1970, it increased more than sevenfold to about 300 million pounds per year. Some other examples of increases in annual pollutant output since 1946: nitrogen oxides from automobiles (which trigger the formation of smog), 630 per cent; tetraethyl lead from gasoline, 415 per cent; mercury from chloralkali plants, 2,100 per cent; synthetic pesticides (between 1950 and 1957 only), 270 per cent; inorganic nitrogen fertilizer (some of which leaches into surface water and pollutes it), 789 per cent; nonreturnable beer bottles, 595 per cent. Many pollutants were totally absent before World War II, having made their environmental debut in the war years: smog (first noticed in Los Angeles in 1943), man-made radioactive elements (first produced in the wartime atomic bomb project), DDT (widely used for the first time in 1944), detergents (which began to displace soap in 1946), synthetic plastics (which became a contributor to the rubbish problem only after the war). (*The Closing Circle*, p. 128)

This paragraph has more than one topic; it turns from phosphates to "other examples." It also contains numerous statistics. Thus it would be difficult to write a short, meaningful note in the margin. Instead, the most important facts have been underlined; an important sentence has been marked with a bar (|); and an interesting detail has been marked with a bracket (⟨).

Reading specialists do not necessarily recommend underlining. Many readers will underline two-thirds of a paragraph; in such cases, the activity becomes automatic, just as moving the eyes without seeing the words is automatic. Moreover, if it is done carefully (with a ruler), it takes our time and attention away from the author.

It is therefore likely that, in general reading, little more than the topic sentence would be underlined—and sometimes only part of that sentence:

The widespread suspicion and even hostility of businessmen to government, even when, as in the case of the Eisenhower Administration, it was presumptively sympathetic to business, is one of the great constants in our political life.

In technical reading, only the outstanding facts should be so marked. Underlining is used sparingly in the second Commoner passage, to mark the major statement on phosphates, the outstanding statistic of pollution increase (mercury from chloralkali plants), and the list of post-World War II pollutants. The bar and brackets show connecting ideas.

Readers will, of course, design their own systems for marking. One more model may be provided for guidance, however. It is a marked essay by Commoner titled "The Second Law of Ecology: Everything Must Go Somewhere." Try to read all of it before reviewing the marks.

> This is, of course, simply a somewhat informal restatement of a basic law of physics—that matter is indestructible. Applied to ecology, the law emphasizes that in nature there is no such thing as "waste." In every natural system, what is excreted by one organism as waste is taken up by another as food. Animals release carbon dioxide as a respiratory waste; this is an essential nutrient for green plants. Plants excrete oxygen, which is used by animals. Animal organic wastes nourish the bacteria of decay. Their wastes, inorganic materials such as nitrate, phosphate, and carbon dioxide, become algal nutrients.

> A persistent effort to answer the question "Where does it go?" can yield a surprising amount of valuable information about an ecosystem. Consider, for example, the fate of a household item which contains mercury—a substance with serious environmental effects that have just recently surfaced. A dry-cell battery containing mercury is purchased, used to the point of exhaustion, and then "thrown out." But where does it really go? First it is placed in a container of rubbish; this is collected and taken to an incinerator. Here the mercury is heated; this produces mercury vapor which is emitted by the incinerator stack, and mercury *vapor* is toxic. Mercury vapor is carried by the wind, eventually brought to earth in rain or snow. Entering a mountain lake, let us say, the mercury condenses and sinks to the bottom. Here it is acted on by bacteria which convert it to methyl mercury. This is soluble and taken up by fish; since it is not metabolized, the mercury accumulates in the organs and flesh of the fish. The fish is caught and eaten by a man and the mercury becomes deposited in his organs, where it might be harmful. And so on.

> This is an effective way to trace out an ecological path. It is also an excellent way to counteract the prevalent notion that something which is regarded as useless simply "goes away" when it is discarded. Nothing "goes away"; it is simply transferred from place to place, converted from one molecular form to another, acting on the life processes of any organism in which it becomes, for a time, lodged. One of the chief reasons for the present environmental crisis is that great amounts of materials have been extracted from the earth, converted into new forms, and discharged into the environment without taking into account that "everything has to go somewhere." The result, too often, is the accumulation of harmful amounts of material in places where, in nature, they do not belong. (*The Closing Circle*, pp. 39–41)

Note that nothing is underlined in the second paragraph, and very little is underlined elsewhere. When paragraphs are transitional, or parenthetical, few marks should be made.

Summary

Active reading means responding to the writer's ideas. Marginal notes may or may not be practical; readers should devise their own shorthand systems for marking the important ideas in a text.

Chapter 8

Modes of Reduction

In reciting—reviewing what we have learned from a reading selection—
we are advised to write at more length. Now notes are put together, so
that a synthesis of the author's ideas emerges. Facts may be memorized,
but facts serve ideas; it is the author's theory, or theories, which above all
must be retained.

The synthesizing process may be called reduction. It involves the
removal of inessential material until only a valuable core remains—just
as miners extract a few pounds of valuable metal from tons of earth and
rock. The ability to get to "the heart of the matter" is itself a priceless
quality, perhaps because it is rare. Papers are too long, meetings run too
long, and mistakes in communications are made, all because too few
writers and speakers can arrive quickly at central issues.

The discussion here centers on means of reducing ideas to their core, in
writing. There are basically four such means. The first of them—outlining—is considered an inefficient method of recitation in the reading
process; it will be discussed as a writing tool in Chapter 9. The other three
are writing modes, called here "modes of reduction."

Figure 5 illustrates the functions of these modes. These functions are
also the subject of the sections which follow.

Definitions

Sometimes the key to understanding a reading passage lies in the
definition of a crucial term. This is less often the case in technical writing
than in general writing; definitions are important enough, however, that
all nonnative professional men and women should know how to construct
them.

Words have, of course, dictionary definitions, which are universal and
historical (because the words are traced to their roots). Such definitions

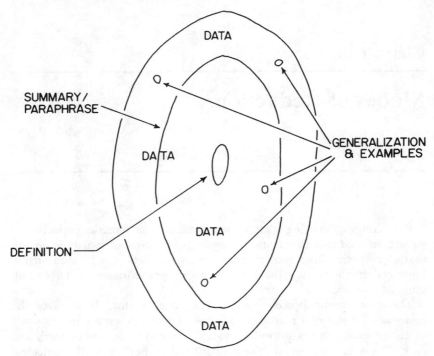

FIG. 5. *Modes of reduction.*

tend to be short, relying heavily on synonyms. At most, they place a word into a class, and then distinguish it from other members of the class:

> *skunk* (skunk), n. (contr. Am. Ind. [Abnaki] *segonku*). . . . 1) . . . a bushy-tailed mammal about the size of a cat; it has glossy black fur, usually with white stripes down its back, and ejects an offensive-smelling, musky liquid when molested. . . . (*Webster's New World Dictionary of the American Language: College Edition*)

Sometimes old words are used in new ways, however; such is the case with Galbraith's use of *affluent,* as we shall see. Moreover, new terms are constantly being invented, and they require expanded definitions. Sometimes examples are also appropriate to help others understand the term. At other times—when the term denotes a process—a working definition is required. Here is Commoner's definition of *cybernetics*:

> The word "cybernetics" derives from the Greek word for helmsman; it is concerned with cycles of events that steer, or govern, the

behavior of a system. The helmsman is part of a system that also includes the compass, the rudder, and the ship. If the ship veers off the chosen compass course, the change shows up in the movement of the compass needle. Observed and interpreted by the helmsman this event determines a subsequent one: the helmsman turns the rudder, which swings the ship back to its original course. When this happens, the compass needle returns to its original, on-course position and the cycle is complete. If the helmsman turns the rudder too far in response to a small deflection of the compass needle, the excess swing of the ship shows up in the compass—which signals the helmsman to correct his overreaction by an opposite movement. Thus the operation of this cycle stabilizes the course of the ship. (*The Closing Circle*, pp. 33–34)

To understand the term *cybernetics* is to understand the central idea of Commoner's book.

As a form of recitation, a definition is even more appropriate with Galbraith's book. Galbraith does not himself suggest a definition for his term *affluent society*. The term is widely used now, but only because of his book; before Galbraith, one rarely heard the word "affluent."

What does he mean, then, by the "affluent society"? By taking time to give the term a working definition, we comprehend, and retain, his essential ideas. A model follows:

Affluent society. "Affluence" comes from the Latin words *ad-* (to) and *fluere* (flow), and is defined as "flowing freely," "abundant," or "wealthy." Perhaps "affluent" suggests, better than "wealthy," the flow of goods and wealth, but Galbraith himself immediately uses "wealthy" as a synonym. By "society," he means a nation.

Galbraith applies the term "affluent society" to the United States of the last few generations. Its most obvious characteristic is overproduction. Americans believe production solves all problems, but actually it goes beyond meeting real needs to create new needs. The affluent society is also characterized by a false sense of national security, heavy consumer indebtedness, inflation, and inadequate public services.

It will be seen that the synonym "wealthy" is much less helpful than the list of characteristics. A definition such as this, used in recitation, reduces an elaborate theory to a core which can be retained.

Summarizing

As Figure 5 indicates, effective summaries always reduce original passages by half or more. As recitation exercises, they should reduce the original much farther. They should be written in English and in words of the reader's choice; direct quotations do not aid the learning/retaining process for nonnative speakers.

A summary is more than a list of main ideas. Properly done, it is a writing exercise, with paragraphs and connected sentences. The reader must demonstrate control of the author's central idea, rather than control of the "pieces" which make up the idea. As an example, a passage from Georg Borgstrom's *Focal Points* (New York: Macmillan, 1973) is here presented. (Reprinted with permission of Macmillan Publishing Co., Inc. from *Focal Points* by Georg Borgstrom. Copyright © 1971, 1973 by Georg Borgstrom.) Borgstrom writes on world food production and food shortages; here, in a chapter on Canada's ability to increase food production, he considers the potential of Western Canada, where water is not abundant.

> Since the thirties hundreds of millions of dollars have been invested in irrigation, and the era when this could be paid for by the farmers themselves is long since past. Big-scale investments from public tax money are now required. Some of the largest irrigation projects on earth are found in these regions. The Nelson and Churchill rivers are expected to provide all three prairie provinces with supplementary water. The reservoir for this purpose is located in southern Saskatchewan. The net gain in new acreages is, however, not overly impressive, merely half a million acres. Water for more is not available. . . .
>
> The experts estimate that all of western Canada, i.e., the prairie provinces and British Columbia, the Pacific region, can in the future contribute at the most an additional 7.5 million acres. This means that the present tilled acreage of this region would increase by one-seventh. But for at least one-third of these new lands considerable capital would be necessary for irrigation and drainage.
>
> The water shortage may appear paradoxical since Canada has within its borders one-third of the globe's freshwater resources, even more than Siberia, thanks to the numerous lakes. The total flow of the rivers is larger than that of all rivers in the United States, Alaska included. It is therefore no mere coincidence that the United States is casting covetous glances at Canada's water resources, even regarding them as future insurance. The Canadians resent this, the more so since they have become increasingly aware of the large future needs of their own country: these water resources are indispensable for further industrial and agricultural development. Nonetheless, water may in time emerge as Canada's most important export item. With water-squandering United States rapidly approaching a crisis, a great deal supports this speculation. The United States is already Canada's most important customer and the recipient of close to nine-tenths of its exported fish, nearly all its paper pulp, large quantities of its timber, and now its natural gas, supplied by pipelines from recently discovered fields in Alberta. (*Focal Points*, pp. 101–102)

The preceding passage might be summarized as follows:

Model Summary

Western Canada has huge, publicly financed irrigation projects, which add only 500,000 acres to cultivation. In all, these provinces can add only one-seventh to their present tilled acreage, and then only with extensive irrigation. Ironically, Canada as a whole has tremendous freshwater resources, which already interest the United States and which may become a Canadian export item.

Two categories of information are usually left out of a summary. First, there are few statistics—in this case, only the most important two. Second, information which does not concern the major idea (Canada's resources) is omitted; thus, the United States and its role as Canada's main customer are minimized.

Through these omissions, the original 342 words have been reduced to 58, or by five-sixths.

Generalization and Examples

Whereas a summary avoids details, a recitation in generalization-and-examples form would seek them out. It is true that a theory must be supported; thus the reader/writer finds a few memorable examples, or "proofs." A model is provided below, again from the chapter on Canada in *Focal Points*. Here Borgstrom is discussing Ontario's potential.

The experts are by and large in agreement that eastern Canada has reached its limits for agricultural development. With increasing population, agriculture has gradually been intensified. Grain production moved to the prairie expanses and the East started intense production of milk, meat, fruits, and vegetables. The Ontario basin is the richest region with first-rate soils, high yields, and a flourishing agricultural economy.

But the picture is not altogether rosy.... The recreational areas for city dwellers are shrinking. The tilled acreage reached its largest extension as early as 1921. Since then the breaking of new lands has not kept pace with the loss of land to cities, industries, airfields, etc., and even the most optimistic experts doubt that there is much soil left suitable for tilling. Marginal lands, that is, soils too poor to yield a reasonable return, were put under the plow long ago. The old people on the farms can relate how the rivulets and streams, which in their youth were filled with water, have vanished forever. The disappearance of hundreds of miles of such waters during the past fifty years is recorded in various surveys. Primarily forest devastation and secondly higher acre-yields, requiring a larger share of the precipitation, are the root causes of this phenomenon. The most severe current threat, however, is water pollution by industries and cities, spreading chemicals and disease agents to the detriment of people, animals, and crops. It all sounds very familiar.

Even many segments of the magnificent St. Lawrence Seaway are heavily polluted. The Great Lakes, especially Lake Michigan and Lake Erie, are rapidly being converted into sewage recipients. Many rivers, discharging into these lakes, are shockingly loaded with all kinds of refuse from industries and the congested population. (*Focal Points*, pp. 94–95)

The generalization-and-examples approach yields the following:

General Idea: Ontario's agriculture has reached its limits and faces trouble ahead.
Example 1:   Basically, all tillable land has been in use since 1921.
Example 2:   Hundreds of miles of rivers have dried up.
Example 3:   Lake Michigan, Lake Erie, and the St. Lawrence Seaway have been polluted.

A summary would have taken account of the topic in the first paragraph while excluding details like "1921." The generalization-and-examples exercise has room for only one idea, however. As recitation, it prepares the reader for active use of what has been read, in debate, conference presentation, or writing of his or her own.

Written out in paragraph form, in fact, the exercise would almost conform to the model of a paragraph presented earlier in this unit. Moreover, it would conform to the traditional thesis-and-support format of expository writing in English, which will be discussed in the next chapter.

Summary

The modes of reduction are means of converting passive knowledge to active knowledge. The one chosen as the appropriate recitation exercise depends on the information read and on the use the writer wishes to make of it.

Further Reading

American Heritage Dictionary. New York: Dell, 1980.

Byrd, Patricia, Carol A. Drum, and Barbara Jean Wittkopf. *Guide to Academic Libraries in the United States.* Englewood Cliffs, N.J.: Prentice-Hall, 1981.

Dubin, Fraida, and Elite Olshtain. *Reading By All Means: Reading Improvement Strategies for English Language Learners.* Reading, Mass.: Addison-Wesley Publishing Co., 1981.

Lapedes, Daniel N., ed. *McGraw-Hill Dictionary of Scientific and Technical Terms.* New York: McGraw-Hill, 1978.

Mackay, Ronald, Bruce Barkman, and R. R. Jordan, eds. *Reading in a Second Language.* Rowley, Mass.: Newbury House, 1979.

Markstein, Linda, and Louise Hirasawa. *Expanding Reading Skills: Advanced.* Rowley, Mass.: Newbury House, 1977.

Morgan, Clifford T., and James Deese. *How to Study.* New York: McGraw-Hill, 1969.

Robinson, Francis P. *Effective Reading.* New York: Harper & Brothers, 1962.

Sonka, Amy L. *Skillful Reading.* Englewood Cliffs, N.J.: Prentice-Hall, 1981.

PART III

BASIC PRINCIPLES
IN WRITING ENGLISH

OBJECTIVES

- To describe the natural parts of a composition
- To classify and describe logical modes of organization
- To review principles of coherence and control

English has been a written language for more than 1,000 years. Out of that long history have come set ideas about both the structure and the process of a piece of writing. These ideas are constantly challenged, and experimented with, by the millions of people on all continents who today write in English. Skillful writers can always bend the rules of English writing to suit their purposes.

Nevertheless, there are a few generally accepted principles in the Anglo-American tradition of writing. Expository prose—that is, the essay, the article, the memorandum, and even notes for a speech—should have (according to this tradition) three parts. Its major sections should be organized according to established rhetorical modes (see Figure 6 in Chapter 10). Finally, it should have the qualities of completeness, simplicity, balance, and relevance.

It is the purpose of this section to review these basic principles, and to provide exercises which will reinforce them.

Chapter 9

The Three-Part Composition

Basic principles are easier to state than to implement. So it is with the three-part composition. The three parts—the beginning, the middle, and the end—are too easily said, for they seem obvious.

It is more helpful to think of these three parts as the introduction, the body, and the conclusion, and to remember a definition known by every English teacher. The three parts, according to this definition, are intended (1) "to tell them what you're going to tell them"; (2) "to tell them"; and (3) "to tell them what you've told them." In reality each part has a more complicated function.

The Introduction

The chief feature of the introduction is that it makes broad statements; it is not concerned with small details. It is often described as a passage which answers the general questions, who? what? where? and when? More specifically, it has three functions, which may be called (1) identifying, (2) interesting, and (3) focusing.

Identifying the subject. Before two strangers can converse meaningfully, they must be introduced. Similarly, your readers must know, precisely, your subject before they can follow your thoughts.

Interesting the reader. A good writer knows his or her audience and how to get its attention. Your writing is useless unless you make the subject seem interesting to the reader, and this task should be accomplished in the introduction.

Focusing on the structure. As it moves toward the body of the paper, the introduction appropriately gives a structural signal—a sign of the approach, or rhetorical mode, which follows. For example, the statement

61

"Postal rates may be divided into four categories," placed at the end of the introduction, indicates the structure of the body (in this case, a classification).

The Body

The basic structure for expository prose is often referred to as "thesis and support." Clearly, the introduction must state the thesis—the main idea—whereas the support comes in the body. This means that the body (1) is the longest part of the composition, and (2) contains the details.

Because the body is long, it must be divided into parts; because it is full of details, they must be arranged for the reader's understanding. Systems have therefore been developed to organize supporting details, the best known being the scientific method of classification. An example follows, from a botany text (H. A. Gleason, *Plants of the Vicinity of New York*, New York: Hafner Press, 1962, p. 32):

I. WOODY PLANTS

1a. Trees, with a well-developed trunk and reaching heights of more than 6 m. (20 feet); young trees of smaller size rarely produce flowers and those that do may be sought either here or through *1b—2.*

1b. Shrubs, usually without a single well-developed trunk, blooming and bearing fruit when less than 6 m. tall—*132.*

    2a. Key for trees bearing leaves but no flowers—*3.*

    2b. Key for trees bearing flowers but no leaves—*44.*

    2c. Key for trees bearing both flowers and leaves—*59.*

    2d. Key for trees with fruits—*89.*

3a. Leaves needle-like or scale-like, or awl-shaped or linear, less than 5 mm. wide, mostly (all but one) evergreen—*4.*

3b. Leaves flat, certainly more than 5 mm. wide, mostly (all but two) falling in autumn—*5.*

    4a. Leaves distinctly alternate or scattered or in bundles or fascicles, always at least 10 mm. long (Pine, Tamarack, Spruce, Hemlock)   **Pinaceae**, p. 108

    4b. Leaves distinctly opposite or whorled (in trees with small appressed leaves this character must be looked for carefully) (Cedar, White Cedar, Juniper, Arbor Vitae)

\   **Cupressaceae**, p. 108

The botanist has so many details to organize that he constantly shifts subcategories ahead; note the references to new categories, or new page numbers, at the end of each line. The writer or speaker organizing general materials traditionally uses a less complex system:

I. Introduction: Statement of central idea

II. Supporting detail 1
   A. Category 1 (of Supporting detail 1)
   B. Category 2
      1. Subcategory 1 (of Category 2, Supporting detail 1)
      2. Subcategory 2
         a. Sub-subcategory 1 (of IIB2)
         b. Sub-subcategory 2
         c. Sub-subcategory 3
   C. Category 3
III. Supporting detail 2
   A. Category 1 (of Supporting detail 2)
   etc.

Unlike botanists, writers make outlines only for themselves, not for the reader, and many good writers do not go through the outlining process. Doing so is helpful to the inexperienced writer, however. The outline above represents the logic of effective organization: dividing an idea into parts, the parts into smaller parts, and so on.

The "parts" usually become paragraphs for the reader, for one function of a new paragraph is to announce a new idea. The supporting detail noted in two or three words beside the Roman numeral may be written into a topic sentence. For example, let us assume we are outlining a memo which argues for the purchase of a new wrench:

I. Intro: New wrench should be purchased
II. Adaptable to all sizes

The heading beside II might become the topic sentence, "First, the wrench will adapt to all sizes of piping, from the smallest tubes to the very largest pipes." The paragraph would be completed by the "smaller parts" placed under II in the outline.

The paragraph would then have the "thesis and support" structure which is considered ideal in English expository prose. Once the idea has been sufficiently supported, or developed, a new idea is presented in a new paragraph, with another topic sentence. The old idea and the new idea must be related logically, however, as will be discussed in Chapters 10 and 11.

The Conclusion

The three parts of the composition are closely related. The connection between the introduction and the conclusion is thematic: The conclusion should return to the general idea expressed at the beginning of the composition. That is, the paper correctly ends on the central idea, *not* on a detail.

The conclusion has two functions. First, it signals to the reader that the presentation has been completed. Second, it gives the reader a message to take away. There are several forms that can be used to accomplish these functions:

Restatement.   The conclusion should never repeat exactly words used in the introduction, but it may state the same idea in new words. For example, the focusing statement, "Policy A appears to be better than Policy B for the following reasons," may be echoed in the conclusion as "In view of these facts, I recommend that we adopt Policy A."

Findings and recommendations.   A long report will require a long conclusion, and will probably treat a problem which requires a solution. Professional reports typically conclude with organized statements of the facts discovered by the writer in the course of his or her research, followed by recommendations for action.

Summary.   When the writer merely reports without recommending, a summary of major ideas may be appropriate. It is *not* appropriate in a short report, where the reader can remember the main idea. Rather, it is useful when the composition has dealt at length with complicated ideas or materials.

Deflectors.   Because the conclusion depends heavily on what has preceded it, several other alternatives are possible. Among these are deflectors which tend to relieve the reader from a concentration on details. Possible deflectors are the humorous remark, the story which illustrates the point, and the quotation of an authority. Another possibility was illustrated in Chapter 6, where we saw Professor Galbraith deflect our attention at the end of a section of *The Affluent Society* with a one-sentence paragraph:

> There will be occasion presently for a further word on the competition between the businessman and the intellectual for contemporary esteem.

This is a transitional paragraph—neither the book nor even the chapter has ended—but it is also a conclusion.

Summary

The three parts of the composition are closely connected but have distinctive purposes. The writer confuses—or loses—the reader if each part does not perform its expected functions.

Chapter 10

Rhetorical Modes

Writers in the Anglo-American tradition attempt to follow a straight line in developing their ideas; their paragraphs, both internally and collectively, are meant to move in a single direction. This ideal cannot always be met because certain rhetorical modes require changes in direction, but it indicates the efficiency readers in English-speaking cultures will expect of professional persons who write.

Efficiency means an economy in writing. Professional presentations are not valued for the sound of the words or (usually) for the play of subtle ideas, but rather for the expression of clear ideas as briefly as possible. Most writers feel that good organization leads to such brevity, principally because, by organizing well, they eliminate repetition. Several basic patterns of organization, known as the "rhetorical modes," have been developed over the years; they are shown in Figure 6 and are described below.

Modes of Reduction

The modes of reduction—definition, summary, and generalization and examples—were introduced in Chapter 8. Unlike the other rhetorical modes, they perform functions rather than provide structures. They do not aim for active, thorough coverage of a topic, and among them, only the generalization-and-examples mode consistently contains a body organized by the writer. Accordingly, they will not be considered further here.

Modes of Division

Two rhetorical modes are distinguished by their natural complexity. Either they deal with more than one subject, or they deal with one

65

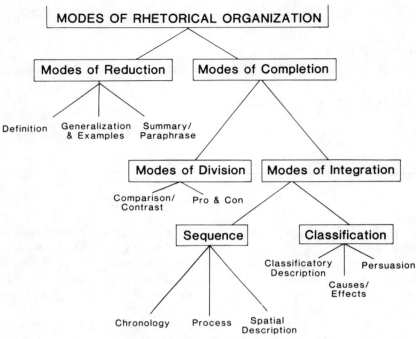

FIG. 6. *Rhetorical modes.*

subject—an issue—from conflicting points of view. Literal "straight-line" development is impossible, but there are various strategies for developing ideas efficiently.

Comparison/contrast.   Two or more subjects may be reviewed for their similarities, for their differences, or for both. As an example, assume that we are comparing two companies for the purpose of determining which provides the better investment opportunity. Our considerations would include current profits, market potential, labor supply, and management efficiency. The analysis might be outlined as follows:

    I. Current profits
        A. Company A
        B. Company B
    II. Market potential
        A. Company A
        B. Company B
        etc.

We are organizing our presentation, in short, around the variables (factors which change) by which companies may be judged. On the other hand, it is equally logical to deal with each company in turn:

I. Company A
    A. Current profits
    B. Market potential
    C. Labor supply
    D. Management efficiency
II. Company B
    A. Current profits
    B. Market potential
    C. Labor supply
    D. Management efficiency

Still a third approach is possible, when we find that there are many similarities between the two subjects but also important differences. Let us assume that we find the two companies very much alike on the variables listed above, but Company A has a much newer physical plant and much less long-term debt. The structure of our analysis might be this:

I. Similarities
    A. Current profits
    B. Market potential
    C. Labor supply
    D. Management efficiency
II. Differences
    A. Physical plant
    B. Long-term debt

Each of these structures has advantages and disadvantages. The writer must choose the one which presents his or her ideas most efficiently.

Pro and con. It is often difficult to distinguish the structure of a pro-and-con paper, which presents opposing positions, from a comparison, particularly when the comparison results in the expression of an opinion or a recommendation. They are most clearly separated on the basis of the number of subjects. The pro-and-con paper properly has a single subject, which is an issue—that is, it deals with attitudes as well as with facts.

Pro-and-con structure is often very simple: The arguments on one side of the issue are taken up first and the arguments on the other side next. Let us assume that the union at an oil refinery has bargained for an 8 percent raise and that the management is considering a 9 percent raise for non-union employees. This is certain to be an issue. The chief personnel ficer might analyze the "pros and cons" in preparing to write a memo to the president:

    I. Reasons why non-union employees should have a large raise
      A. Non-union wages have lagged behind union wages
      B. Non-union employees' productivity is higher
      C. It is important to keep these people happy outside the union
   II. Reasons why non-union employees should *not* have a large raise
      A. The union might organize a strike or slow-down
      B. The current union officers, who have been responsible leaders, might be voted out
      C. A passage in the union contract gives the union grounds to file a complaint with the National Labor Relations Board

Logically, the writer would place the position he or she favors last, where it would lead naturally to the conclusion. In this example, we would assume that the chief personnel officer opposes a large raise for the non-union employes.

Modes of Sequence

The rhetorical structures called "modes of sequence" in Fig. 6 are sometimes referred to as "natural orders," because the materials arrange themselves for the writer. It is here that the ideal of straight-line development is fulfilled.

Chronology. The order of time is the mode of the story, and although stories may not be easy to tell, they are easy to organize. Thus, a historian writing a history of the United States would start at the beginning (1608 or 1776) and would end with the most recent events. For example:

   1.   The colonial era
   2.   The revolutionary era
   3.   The new republic
   4.   Jacksonian democracy
   5.   The Civil War
   etc.

The historian would not, and should not, rearrange these topics—e.g., discuss the Civil War (1861–1865) before the Revolutionary War (1775–1883).

Process. Although it is closely related to chronology, the process mode differs in that steps in a sequence, not units of time, are the basis for the division of the materials. An example of a process paper is the note of instructions or directions which accompanies a product sold to the public. These compositions are (or should be) organized clearly around a set of steps the buyer must take for the proper use of the product. Here are possible instructions for the operation of a new camera:

1. Load film in compartment marked by blue arrow.
2. Shut cover firmly.
3. Turn film until "1" appears in the small window.

    etc.

Again, one would follow the natural order of these steps; reversing them would cause great confusion.

A question does arise, however, when there are as many as 15 or 20 steps. Should they be grouped into "stages" of three or four steps each, or listed individually, perhaps with numbers, as above? For a general audience (the camera-buying public), it is usual to list the individual steps. A more sophisticated audience will expect writers to group the steps into logical clusters.

Spatial description. Writing descriptive passages will not come as easily as writing a chronology-based paper; logically speaking, however, there is little difference. When describing a physical entity—a machine, a building, a park—the writer may start at one point in space and move in a line to the other points in space occupied by that physical entity.

A simple illustration is the caption which accompanies any picture of a group of people in a newspaper. Those in the first row are always named first, starting from the left, then those in the second row (starting again from the left), and so on. A building, similarly, may logically be described in this order: first floor, one end to the other end; second floor, one end to the other; and so on. Generally, English-speaking readers expect organization to move from left to right, as on the printed page. Accordingly , the writer would probably begin the description of the first floor at the left end, which is determined by facing the front of the building.

A final note: Description is not necessarily organized spatially, as the following paragraphs indicate. When the spatial mode is chosen, however, it should not be mixed with another mode.

Modes of Classification

As opposed to natural orders, the logical orders require analysis. The modes of classification are the principal vehicles of analytical writing. To classify, the writer must (1) review all of the data, (2) divide those data into logical categories, and (3) arrange those categories for effective presentation to the reader.

Straight-line development may not seem relevant to classification papers. Good writers, however, always look for a principle by which to arrange their categories. A common solution is to use an order of importance (or size): The writer begins with the least important category and ends with the most important. The reverse—moving from most important to least important—is also possible, depending on the materials being analyzed.

Classificatory description.   The broadest of the rhetorical modes is classificatory description, which organizes facts, ideas, or physical entities into groups, and *organizing these groups is its only purpose.*

Examples of this mode lie close at hand. One is this chapter, with its categories and subcategories of organizational principles. Another—though in a visual form rather than in prose—is Figure 6, which contains a description by type of rhetorical modes. Every company's organization chart is, similarly, a classificatory description.

Although we associate classification with the scientist, much communication outside the sciences also proceeds via classificatory description. This includes the description of physical entities. The building used above as an example of spatial description could also be described by categories—production areas, administrative areas, storage areas, and so forth—without any reference to spatial arrangement.

Analysis.   Dictionary definitions for "classification" and "analysis" are virtually the same. The words mean the process of breaking a large, complex entity into its parts. To the modern speaker of English, however, analysis implies a search for either the causes of a problem or the effects of a real or possible action.

The chemist's hypothesis and the technician's inspection of a broken machine are both steps in analysis. The technician may find several causes for the breakdown, only one cause, or one original cause which set off a chain reaction. The chemist's predictions of effects have the same three possibilities. Often the chemist will prove a prediction wrong, and the technician often will not know with certainty whether the cause(s) of the breakdown has been identified correctly.

Analysis is, therefore, hard mental labor. The presentation of the analytic process on paper, however, is simple. When writers wish to speak of chain reactions, they organize around steps, as in the process mode. When they wish to speak of causes not related to each other, they properly discuss each in turn. There is no one correct (or straight-line) way to arrange unrelated causes or effects, unless a clear order of importance emerges.

Persuasion.   What has been said about structuring an analysis is true also for structuring an argument. The writer thinks through all of the reasons that support a position, groups them into categories, and presents the categories one by one. A purchasing agent, for example, may see many compelling reasons for changing an account from one supplier to another, and make a case this way:

1. Economic reasons
2. Administrative reasons
3. Public relations reasons

etc.

Here, the most compelling reason would probably be placed last.

Complex Structures

For those who must write professionally, but are not professional writers, the first rule is to adopt a single rhetorical mode and follow it (see Chapter 11). Unfortunately, a long, complex report usually cannot be sustained by one mode. Thus, the second rule is to shift modes, when necessary, with great care, making sure that the reader is not confused.

The best strategy for preventing confusion in such reports is to write a thorough introduction. Obviously, writers must plan complex compositions before they begin to write them. In the introduction, then, they give their readers signals as to all the structures which will follow. If they intend, for example, both to describe a process and to analyze it, they indicate as much in the introduction. Moreover, when they have finished describing the process, they notify the reader of the switch to analysis.

Figure 7 represents graphically the parts of a complex paper on a proposed merger of "Company X" and "Company Y." As another example, we may take up a writing problem given to engineering students at an American university. The students' assignment is actually to design a small machine; note, however, the variety of rhetorical modes demanded for the Preliminary Design Report:

INSTRUCTIONS FOR PRELIMINARY REPORT

A. *General*

Each student company participating in the design competition will submit one copy of the "Preliminary Design Report" to the section instructor. The function of this report is to communicate (to one unfamiliar with your project) in as concise . . . a form as possible the following information:

1. Project title.

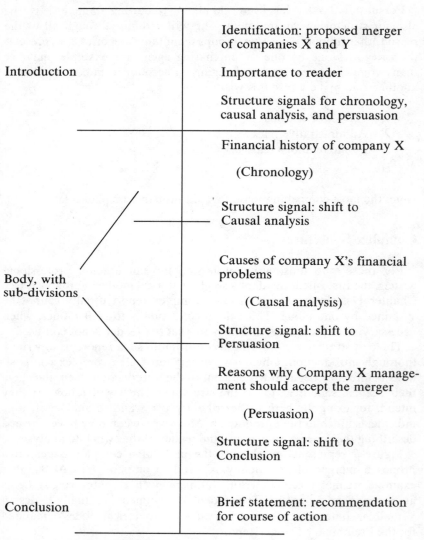

FIG. 7. *Components of a complex writing structure.*

2. Names of participating student engineers.
3. Clear statement of the problem.
4. An analysis of the problem.
5. The alternative solutions that you generated.
6. The particular solution you choose as optimum—and your reasons for this choice.

7. A description of the solution (device, structure, process) which you chose.
8. Any pertinent marketing information . . .
9. All important cost data available to you.
10. Specific recommendations . . .
11. Any other information you feel will enhance the value of your report . . .

As is often the case, some of the required sections force the students to find their own structures; these include items 3 and 11. Others call for differing rhetorical modes: item 4 apparently calls for causal analysis, 5 for classificatory description, 6 for persuasion, and 7 for spatial description. Each shift of mode would require some sort of structure signal.

We shall take up this problem again under the discussion of technical writing (Part IV).

Summary

The rhetorical modes underlie simple, effective writing. Mastery of them is an excellent compensatory skill, for good organization is as important as good grammar in communicating ideas.

Chapter 11

Coherence and Control

More must now be said about the units which together form a rhetorical structure. Several rules have been stated explicitly, or implied, about the nature of these "stages" (in a sequence) and "categories" (in the logical orders), but they have not been applied to all of the rhetorical modes, as they must be. These rules connect the structure of a composition with its content, with its style, and even with its mechanical presentation. They are simple, indeed almost obvious. As may be seen in the exercises for Chapter 11 in Appendix I, however, they are not always easily applied.

Rule 1. Follow one rhetorical mode at a time.

This rule needs repeating, for the reason that inexperienced writers often mix modes, even in short compositions. The description of an assembly line which begins spatially, for example, may easily shift into considerations of functions (inspection points, etc.) and lose its spatial orientation, thus confusing the reader.

Rule 2. Arrange the units in a straight line.

Usually, even in the logical modes, the writer can find an appropriate sequence for the details of the body of the composition. The possibilities include (1) an order of occurrence, (2) an order of importance, (3) an order of magnitude or size, and (4) an order of proximity (nearness). Some principle of arrangement should be established. The benefit to the writer who takes time to plan, and to find the best arrangement before writing, is a smooth flow from point to point.

Rule 3. Begin at a natural or logical starting-point.

It is possible to move in a straight line, but backwards. One might be logically consistent in describing the top floor of a building first and working downward to the bottom, but an English-speaking audience would find this procedure inappropriate.

A more difficult question arises in analysis and persuasion. The logical starting point might seem to be the strongest argument, but this means readers must suffer through weaker arguments as they continue to read, and the paper loses its force. By starting with the weakest point, on the other hand, one may lose the readers' interest immediately. The secret here is to make weak points seem strong, or at least interesting.

Rule 4. Be complete; do not omit important topics.

Chapter 8 identified the modes of reduction as those which intentionally omit details. The structures known in this book as the modes of completion, on the other hand, have as an ideal the thorough coverage of their points, whether units of time, steps in a sequence, arguments for and against a position, or the effects of a proposed action.

The confidence of the audience partly depends upon such thoroughness. We write because we are assumed to be experts; if we fail to make a point which readers know is important, they begin to doubt our expertise. An economist, for example, who writes about the causes of inflation in America and Europe during the 1970's and 1980's without mentioning energy costs would not be considered an expert economist by readers.

Rule 5. Leave out irrelevant material.

The reverse of Rule 4 is the tendency to add materials which don't fit and don't belong. A rhetorical mode is a discipline: It forces the writer to stay within a chosen structure.

Irrelevancy may take several forms, three of which are discussed below.

Personal references. Writers' personalities should not intrude into their prose. Writing in the professions almost always seeks to be objective; the pronoun "I" itself is often avoided, although it may be used to report activities in which "I" is the agent. Personal stories, and particularly the expression of personal feelings, are the real problems. Often, opinions are not only irrelevant but seem offensive to the reader.

Overcompleteness. If there are six strong reasons for requesting a new secretarial position in the office, the manager should not offer more; the seventh and eighth—and particularly the ninth or tenth—reasons will fatigue the vice-president who reads the report. It is possible to be thorough without being tedious.

Failures of control.   The greatest danger of irrelevancy comes from the writer's lack of control over his or her theme, structure, and personal interest. Assume that you are asked to give an evaluation, in writing, of three external candidates for the directorship of company laboratories, and you discover that one of them shares your love of antique cars; assume further that you then write a report which contains only one paragraph each about the other two candidates but two pages about the person you like, one of which deals only with this person's interesting hobby.

Clearly, you have lost control of the assignment, which was to evaluate the candidate's competence. The example is extreme, but it is typical of the ratio between relevant and irrelevant materials in much writing.

Rule 6. Give equal weight to equal ideas and unequal weight to unequal ideas.

The example cited above as a failure of control contains a flaw in addition to irrelevancy. When the page about antique cars is subtracted, the remainder still contains a full page about one candidate and only one *paragraph* about each of the other two. This may be called a failure in balance.

Balance is a matter of both style and space. In some cases "equal weight" means "equal space"—the same number of lines or paragraphs. When an evaluation of three candidates could affect the careers of all three, each should be given roughly equal coverage. Similarly, a review of pros and cons requires us to devote almost as much space to the viewpoint we dislike as to our own.

The opposite problem lies in the consideration of clearly unequal ideas. The tenth argument, as stated earlier, may be omitted, but the seventh, eighth, and ninth perhaps deserve brief mention. Similarly, a sequence may contain a small step which is not essential but cannot be entirely neglected; or, among several clear causes of a problem, there may be one which has a 5 percent chance of being the principal cause; or a classification may include one subcategory which has little importance but must be noted if the classification is to be complete.

How are these small details gathered into the paper? In the Anglo-American tradition, good writers will mention them in passing—a phrase in the introduction, a clause in a long sentence devoted to a more important detail, a rhetorical question in the conclusion. Inexperienced writers would be best advised to group several small details into one paragraph. When there is only one small detail, they must add it as best they can, but briefly.

Rule 7. Do not allow units to overlap.

A common result of the writer's failure to plan carefully is overlap, or repetition. That is, ideas are mentioned in one section of a paper when they clearly should be covered in a different section, or they are repeated because the sections have not been divided cleanly into separate themes. The sections (or categories), in other words, should be *mutually exclusive*.

As an example of overlap, here is the outline of a report listing reasons *not* to invest in Company A:

    I. Introduction
   II. Management inflexibility
      A. Refused to invest in cost-cutting machine
      B. Failed to recognize union needs, which led to strike
  III. Market problems
      A. Company B lowered price of competing product
      B. Company A sales staff was not aggressive
      C. Inflation's effects on consumers were not foreseen
  IV. Labor troubles
      A. Workers complained of shop conditions
      B. Union struck over lack of management concessions
   V. Conclusion

The categories look logical: II, III, and IV all express good reasons not to invest in Company A. Subcategories IIB and IVB, however, express the same idea—they overlap. Possibly either II or IV could be eliminated; at least, they need to be placed together in a straight line and made mutually exclusive.

Summary

This chapter, like Chapters 9 and 10, has stated ideals for effective organization. The hard realities of organizing a mass of random data will be made easier by applying the ideals as rules.

Further Reading

Barnes, Gregory A. *Crisscross: Structured Writing in Context.* Englewood Cliffs, N.J.: Prentice-Hall, 1981.

Jacobi, Ernst. *Writing at Work: Dos, Don'ts, and How Tos.* Rochelle Park, N.J.: Hayden Book Company, Inc., 1976.

Kirszner, Laurie G., and Stephen R. Mandell. *Basic College Writing.* New York: Norton, 1978.

Perrin, Porter G., and Wilma R. Ebbitt. *Writer's Guide and Index to English.* Glenview, Ill.: Scott, Foresman and Company, 1972.

Strunk, William, Jr., and E. B. White. *The Elements of Style.* New York: The Macmillan Company, 1959.

Sullivan, Kathleen E. *Paragraph Practice.* New York: The Macmillan Company, 1971.

Swales, John. *Writing Scientific English.* London: Thomas Nelson & Sons, 1971.

PART IV

GUIDELINES FOR WRITING IN THE PROFESSIONS

OBJECTIVES

- To introduce the standard forms of technical writing
- To encourage objectivity in the presentation of ideas
- To discuss the role of visual information in writing
- To outline a strategy for publishing

The twentieth century is an electronic age, but beyond this, it is the Age of the Information Explosion. Despite the telephone and electronic media, professionals do more writing for one another than ever before. The number of books in print doubles within decades; the number of professional articles has grown so large that certain journals publish only abstracts, not the articles themselves.

This part analyzes professional, or technical, writing—its forms, its content, and its tone. There are three important forms, each with its own conventions, in everyday professional life: business letters, memoranda, and reports. They are the subjects of Chapter 12. Chapter 13 considers the appropriate tone of such documents and, specifically, the avoidance of subjectivity.

Chapter 14 addresses the means by which technical writers convey information visually, through tables, graphs, charts, and many other types of "figures." Finally, in Chapter 15, suggestions are made for turning research ideas into publishable work.

Chapter 12

Standard Forms

The types and purposes of communications generated by people who work professionally are too numerous to be described at length here. This chapter cannot substitute for the books on technical writing which have appeared in recent years; two such books are listed at the end of this part. Nevertheless it can identify, and discuss briefly, three forms of writing which everyone who works in a professional role must generate at some time. These are the business letter, the memorandum, and the report.

Business Letters

The business letter is a communication to the outside world; more specifically, it communicates with a professional person outside the writer's own organization. The letter may simply accompany another document, such as a purchase order, or it may contain a crucial appeal— for a job (as in a letter of application), for a contract worth millions of dollars, or for important political action.

The ability to write good business letters, therefore, is extremely useful. Professional people usually write many such letters, for many purposes. Almost always the *form* of the letter is the same, however; in addition, there are common qualities of correct tone.

Form. The American business letter is always typewritten on 8½ by 11 inch bond paper. There should be white space on all sides of the text, and the text should sit in the center of the page (Fig. 8). Single-spacing is proper, except that a blank line is left between paragraphs and between the various parts of the letter described below. Finally, an indentation of 5 to 10 type spaces begins each paragraph, unless the employing organization requires "block" form—that is, starting all parts of the letter at the left-hand margin.

JOSEPH M. LAMBERT / Consulting Engineer

110 Bala Avenue, Bala Cynwyd, Pa. 19004 (215) 667-5064

February 2, 1981

Stuart A. Kessler, R.I.B.A.
Architect & Planner
654 Madison Avenue
New York, NY 10021

Re: Haddington Housing for Elderly
     Philadelphia, Pennsylvania
     P.H.F.A. Project No. R-813-8E

Gentlemen:

At the job conference of Thursday, January 29, 1981, the General
Contractor advised us that the elevator sub-contractor would not deliver the elevator door frames as scheduled. Therefore, it will be
necessary to introduce steel framine to replace the masonry
construction at the elevator doors. This will permit the General
Contractor to proceed without delay.

Refer to our drawing "Structural Work Sheet - Drawing No. WS-1 -
Dated 1/29/81," for the additional steel framing.

The extra cost for this work will be absorbed by the elevator
sub-contractor.

Sincerely yours,

J.M. Lambert, P.E.

JML:stb

FIG. 8. *Example of a business letter. [Reprinted by permission of Joseph M.
Lambert, P.E.]*

The eight parts of the letter are identified below (see also Figure 8).

1. *Heading.*   The reader must know the return address of the writer.
Letterhead stationery solves this problem; when using stationery without
a letterhead, the writer must give his or her street address and (on a new
line) city, state, and zip code. Except in letters using block form, this
information is placed just to the right of the center of the page. Below it,
the date must appear, with the month written out—for example, October
12, 1982 (British: 12 October 1982); 10/12/82 is incorrect, and confusing.

2. *Inside address.*   Below the heading, and at the left-hand margin, the
recipient's address is written, exactly as it is written on the envelope.

Always give the recipient a title, even if the two of you are on a first-name basis: *Mr.* for men, and *Ms.* for women (unless you know that a woman prefers *Miss* or *Mrs.*). Naturally, if the person has earned a title—Doctor, Reverend, Professor, Dean, Captain, Rabbi, Senator, Judge, etc.—you would use that title or its abbreviation. Normally, you would also list the person's position—for example, Service Manager—after his or her name.

3. *Reference line.* Sometimes a letter addressed to a company will contain a line referring the letter to an appropriate officer, or identifying the subject. For clarity's sake, this line should be placed toward the right-hand side of the page, under the date.

4. *Salutation.* The greeting to the reader appears at the left margin two lines below the inside address, or the reference line if one is used. The first word should be "Dear"; the second word should be the title (Mr., Rev., Mayor, etc.); the third and last should be the person's last name. Of course, personal acquaintances can be addressed by first names: "Dear Charlie," "Dear Margaret," etc. Often, however, the recipient will be unknown by either name or sex. He or she is simply, "Manager, Acme Products." Some writers will therefore greet the recipient as "Dear Manager" or even as "Dear Acme Products." In such cases it is probably best to use the more personal "Dear Sir/Madam." The salutation is followed by a colon.

5. *Text.* Little needs to be said here about the text, except that it begins two lines below the salutation and occupies the center of the page.

6. *Complimentary close.* Two lines below the text, and near the center of the page, the letter is closed with the words "Sincerely yours"; "Very truly yours" is also acceptable. A warmer term, such as "Cordially," is appropriate only for close acquaintances.

7. *Signature block.* Four or five lines below the complimentary close and directly underneath it, the writer's professional name appears; directly under the name comes the professional position, if appropriate. The letter should be signed between the complimentary close and the signature block.

8. *Addenda.* Sometimes information is added after the signature block. This information includes the capitalized initials of the letter writer and the lowercase initials of the typist (e.g., RIJ/las); a reference to enclosed materials, usually written "(Encl.)" or "Enclosures (3)"; or a postscript (added note), which begins with "P.S." All these addenda begin at the left-hand margin.

Again, variations of these conventions may be required by the employing organization.

Content and Style. All manuscript conventions are courtesies to the reader, but it will be noted that the business letter is explicitly courteous: Titles are used, the word "Dear" precedes the recipient's name (even when the writer is angry), and the words "Sincerely yours," at the end, are an assurance of good intentions. Courtesy is more important in a business letter, in fact, than in any other form of writing.

This is not to say that a letter should be flattering or flowery. It is possible to be firm and still be courteous, to say "no" and still be pleasant. Usually the letter is addressed to a representative of another organization, who is simply doing a job. This person cannot respond to either flattery or attack. Even if he or she is responsible for a problem, an angry letter will be ineffective in getting it solved.

Thus the content of the letter should be expressed as pleasantly and as briefly as possible. The letter begins with a clear statement of the problem and ends with the recommended action. Paragraphs should be kept short and right on the topic; jargon (slang words in the profession) or unnecessary technical terms should be avoided.

When the letter has been typed, it should be read for possible errors or unclear words.

Memoranda

The memorandum is the usual form for in-house communication, and the writer often knows the reader(s) personally. Therefore, certain courtesies are omitted, and a different style may be appropriate.

Form. Memoranda should be written on letterhead stationery; a special form is usually provided by the employer. A common design is shown in Figure 9. Note that the memorandum always includes a "subject" line, as well as lines for the sender's and recipient's names. The subject should be stated with the precision of a title (see Appendix III, Grammar Handbook), for memoranda are reference documents: Someone in the company may want to read the memorandum 5 years later and will want to be able to find it quickly.

In some companies memoranda are signed at the bottom, six lines below the text. In other organizations the writer simply initials his or her name on the "From" line.

Content and style. Like business letters, memoranda should come to the point quickly. Too often a memo writer will tell a story rather than draw together the facts. Usually a rhetorical mode *other than chronology* is appropriate. The writer should also keep in mind the principles of

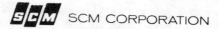

SCM CORPORATION

INTER-OFFICE MEMO

FROM: E. J. Wilson   DATE: November 3, 1980   FOR: C. W. Allen
LOCATION: Phila. #1981

ANSWERING
LETTER OF:

SUBJECT: Heat Recovery Installation

        There are a number of installations which appear to be logical
candidates for recovering heat from the exhaust gases. It is
imperative that we initiate a marketing program to provide such
systems to our customers.

        Some applications are quite clean and require a simple system
of heat exchanger, fans and ductwork. Others involve exhaust gases
containing dust particles which can foul a heat exchanger or volatiles
which can cause corrosion. The latter will require filtering of the
exhaust air and/or special metals to resist corrosion.

        Our first step should be to plan an engineering effort to
establish design parameters and costs. As a parallel effort we can
assess the market potential and establish strategies to sell such
systems. Please give this project your immediate attention and be
prepared to outline a marketing plan early by December 31.

                                            E. J. Wilson
                                          ────────────────
                                            E. J. Wilson

EJW/pm

FIG. 9. *Example of a memorandum. [Reprinted by courtesy of SCM Corporation.]*

control mentioned in Chapter 11, particularly thoroughness, balance, and relevance.

Even more than letters, memos should be efficient and economical. "Shortcuts" are tolerated in memoranda, whereas they may not be appropriate in other writing. Thus, we find abbreviations (e.g., "specs" for "specifications") and symbols like the following:

4'6"	30 mpg
25¢	#2 lead
30°–60° triangle	2 bits @ $1.25 ea.
40%	2 lb. 3 oz.
1.6 m	60 KW
70+ rpm	4" × 4"

Certain function words may also be omitted, particularly articles and prepositions: "Install pole to depth 2'6" and set." In this case, even a pronoun has been left out. In formal English, the sentence would read "Install *the* pole to *a* depth *of* two feet six inches, and set *it*." Such a "clipped" style is not always necessary. Sometimes—particularly when the reader does not work in a technical position—it is inappropriate.

Reports

The least standardized form of technical writing is the report. The reason for its lack of conventions—that is, in a structural sense—is the variety of its purposes. There are dozens of types of reports, from the chemist's laboratory report, to the company president's annual report to stockholders, to the engineer's progress or status report, and each will have its own style as well as its own organization.

These various types are unified by two qualities. The first is a sense of the writer reporting to the reader(s); the reader expects to receive the information, and the writer is professionally obliged to give it. The second quality is the report's "public" nature; it may be quoted, or criticized, or used as a reference, and therefore it must be accurate and well reasoned.

Beyond these characteristics, we can only identify here the special components which may or may not be included.

Letter/memorandum of transmittal.   A cover letter, or memo, is sometimes written to introduce the report. It may remind the reader(s) of the circumstances which generated the report; give information which did not fit into the text itself; add thoughts about the findings; acknowledge the help of others; or simply offer to provide further information and assistance. Such a letter or memorandum gives the writer an opportunity to react personally to the work—that is, to express thoughts which would not be appropriate in the report.

Title page.   The report is usually placed in a cover, even if only a manila folder. When long, and of some importance, it is also preceded by a title page containing the full title and subtitle of the report; the name of the person or organization to which the report is submitted; the name(s) of the report writer(s); the name of any organization providing funds for the research; and the date (at least, the month and the year). The title usually appears again on the first page of the text.

Note that, when a title page is used, it may precede the letter of transmittal.

Table of contents.   In a long report, a table of contents should follow the letter of transmittal. It identifies the major parts of the report, including any appendices. Usually it refers to both headings and sub-headings, in the following format:

Procedure	5
Epoxy Resin Systems	5
Open Spelter Sockets	6
Split-barrel Clamps	8

It should be noted that headings generally replace other transitional devices or structural signals in technical reports. Often they are numbered with Roman numerals.

Abstracts.   Some readers will not read the entire report. Rather, they expect to see, on the first page, a very brief statement of the findings. This statement may be sufficient for their needs or, at least, tell them whether they should keep reading. Thus it is conventional for the writer to provide either an abstract or a summary of the report on the first page.

In business reports, writers increasingly begin with "executive summaries," which generally follow the basic rules for summaries discussed in Chapter 7. To scientists and engineers, however, the word "summary" generally means a summary of conclusions. They use the word "abstract" for a review of a paper's contents.

There are two kinds of abstracts. The "indicative abstract" simply identifies the subject of a paper, and may be very short:

> This report discusses tests made to determine the benefits of using automatic LASER techniques to adjust chip attenuators.

A more helpful form is the "heading (or informative) abstract," which summarizes the problem, the methodology used to address it, and the results.

> The embryotoxicity of hexachlorocyclopentadiene was studied in mice and rabbits. Pregnant animals were given 5, 25, or 75 mg/kg per day by gavage on days 6 to 15 (mice) or 6 to 18 (rabbits) of gestation. Food and water consumption and weight were recorded daily. Mice and rabbit dams were killed on days 18 and 29 of gestation, respectively. Fetuses were removed and examined for malformations. Fertility of the treated mice and rabbits was not significantly different from that of control animals. The dose of 75 mg/kg per day was toxic to rabbit dams; no toxic effects were seen in mice at any dose. No significant effects on the average number of implantations, live fetuses, or resorptions were observed in either species. (from Edward T. Cremmins, *The Art of Abstracting*, Philadelphia: ISI Press, 1982)

Text.   Assuming an abstract has been provided, the text of the report may develop according to the general principles stated in Part III. The introduction announces the subject, notes its importance (by developing the problem), and focuses on the parts to follow. The body is usually several bodies: A progress report might contain a narrative of past work, followed by a process mode to explain work presently in progress, followed by a classification of tasks to be undertaken in the future.

The conclusion returns to the main point, although it is usually expanded to include findings or recommendations. It is also true that some reports state conclusions and recommendations at the beginning. Again, this tells the reader whether it is worthwhile to read the whole report.

Appendices.   Helpful material which is not necessary in the text may be placed at the end of the report, in an appendix. Just as some readers will want the abstract but not the report, others will want the report but not all of the calculations or other evidence. There is always one reader who will inspect all the evidence, however. If technical evidence, contributory facts, or specialized data give essential support to the conclusions, they should be placed in an appendix.

Summary

Throughout their working lives, professionals are called upon to write letters, memoranda, and reports. The last of these are the most complex, requiring skills in both research and organization. Business letters and memoranda form a larger part of daily working life, however, and the ability to write good letters, in particular, may have the most positive benefits on the professional's career.

Chapter 13

Objectivity

> Emotive language is not in itself bad, but when it is information we are after, we shall do well to choose words whose emotive meanings do not distract and hinder us from dealing successfully with what they describe. (Irving M. Copi, *Introduction to Logic*, New York: Macmillan, 1972, p. 71)

All writing contains a point of view. As good readers and good writers both know, printed material is never unbiased truth. Thus, while trying to be objective, the writer must recognize that perfect objectivity cannot be achieved.

Bias is usually present, for example, in our choice of subject. It is probably present in the way we organize our points, particularly when we establish an order of importance for them. In addition, individual words—except strictly technical terms—tend to make the reader see the "facts" from our point of view.

The ideal of objectivity in speaking or writing is, therefore, never quite attainable. Nonetheless, it remains the ideal, and professional workers must strive for it. This chapter briefly deals with three aspects of objectivity (and its opposite, subjectivity). They are tone, loaded words, and emphasis.

Tone

Sometimes an unwanted attitude, or mood, appears in a written or spoken presentation. Here we are not speaking of illogical appeals—to pity, to force, etc.—which are considered logical fallacies (see "Further Reading" at the end of Part IV). The logic used by the presenter may in fact be sound, but an element of emotion or personality is present.

These failures in objectivity may be called problems of tone. Several are described below, as they relate to writing.

Familiarity.   Professional communications normally do not address the audience in a familiar, informal way. Use of the pronouns "I" and "you" is often inappropriate. Examine this statement:

> If you had seen how carefully the maintenance crew worked on that crane, you would know the breakdown wasn't their fault.

This sentence forces the reader to accept the writer's viewpoint. It is too familiar, and too threatening.

Flattery is another example of familiarity. Consider this statement:

> It is clear that this company, and particularly your division, will not tolerate a second-best performance. Under such wise leadership, our efforts will be re-doubled.

Flattery has its benefits, but usually it is inappropriate in formal writing. Familiarity of any sort tends to make the reader uncomfortable. In brief, professional writing is not intended to establish a personal relationship between reader and writer.

Apology.   Sometimes writers lack self-confidence or confidence in their findings. The result can be an uncertainty in their statements which makes a reader skeptical. Here is an example:

> There wasn't really time to inspect the inventory system carefully, and the computer went down just when it was needed. All that can be said is that the inspection team did the best it could.

What reader would believe that the inventory system had been sufficiently well investigated?

Such writing is called apologetic. It does not mean that the writer is personally apologizing for his or her own misdeeds; rather, he or she is expressing regret that the data or the findings are not better.

Apologies appear in many forms:

1.   This point may not seem important to others, but . . .
2.   It is too soon to say these findings are right, but . . .
3.   Some might not agree with these conclusions, but . . .

Such statements may indicate the writer's honesty or modesty, but they do not help in persuading the reader.

Dogmatism.   The opposite of the apology is an insistence on the correctness of one's findings. Note the italicized words below:

1.   *There is no question* that the microprocessor is faulty.
2.   The results show *beyond doubt* that the foreman acted correctly.
3.   The superiority of the Kohler product is *100 percent guaranteed.*

The wise writer knows that there is always a chance for error, that nothing is 100 percent. Yet the principal point is something else: If the data are convincing, they will speak for themselves. The only difference between example 2 and the same sentence *without* "beyond doubt" is that example 2 shows the writer's bias.

Naturally, the writer should also avoid boasting of his or her own expertise:

> As senior Engineer, with more than twenty years' experience, I am the best qualified person to judge the findings.

Like data, expertise will usually speak for itself.

Truculence.   If familiarity makes readers uncomfortable and dogmatism makes them suspicious, a sour attitude will annoy them. Truculence is the attitude of the bad loser:

1. Some people will ignore the facts when it's convenient to do so.
2. A good method was proposed, but unwisely rejected.
3. Since this proposal was not accepted, it must be concluded that our assistance is no longer wanted.

Anger can be seen in these statements—and anger must be avoided (or at least disguised) in professional communications. More will be said on this subject below in the section on "Loaded Words."

Whimsy.   Sometimes humor is useful in technical writing, but whimsy—cute writing—is not. Avoid personal stories, small jokes, puns, and other "cutenesses" which make writing too familiar and casual. Examples demonstrate the point:

1. The explosion nearly made Brown's dentures fall out.
2. The machine now runs as smooth as Sid Wenn's bald head.
3. This saw can cut a perfect curve—better than a Playboy bunny's.

These are not *economical* statements of fact, and in fact they are not relevant (or even amusing).

Loaded Words

Dictionaries do not always tell us everything a word means. They give us a literal reference—a *denotation*—for the word, but often there are connotations as well. Thus the denotation of "ignorant" is "uninformed" or "unknowing," but its connotation is "stupid" or "unthinking"; the word has very negative feelings attached to it. The nonnative speaker must be careful in his or her usage of words with such hidden meanings.

Two categories of words with offensive connotations will be mentioned here: obscene terms and provocative terms.

Obscene terms.   Like all languages, English has numerous slang words for sexual organs and acts, and for body parts and functions. The most specific of them are soon learned and avoided. Others have proper meanings in formal English and may well be used in professional communications, but the nonnative speaker must recognize their connotations.

One can avoid words with obscene connotations by asking a friend for advice. A native speaker will know words which have a proper meaning but also an "improper" meaning.

Provocative terms.   Words which provoke anger or embarrassment cannot be reduced to a short list. There are many ways to insult people, even when we do not intend to insult them. When we challenge an idea, for example, we may seem to be attacking the person behind it. When we call a design "ridiculous," we are likely to offend the designer. *Ridiculous* is, in fact, a good example of a "loaded" word. It may be accurate in a given situation, but it is likely to cause trouble.

Earlier it was stated that anger should be avoided in professional communications, and we are not likely to use words like "ridiculous" unless we are angry. The result of our using it is that our opponent then becomes angry, and good communication stops. Logically, we cannot dismiss our opponent's idea with the word "ridiculous" anyway; it simply raises the question, *why* is the idea ridiculous?

A list of provocative terms to avoid is presented in Table 2. These are terms which in almost any situation will offend the reader or the audience. There are in addition dozens of slang words which are considered inappropriate in formal presentations, and which may in fact be offensive; examples include "goofy" (silly), "chick" (young woman), and "kinky" (eccentric).

Beyond all these, there are terms which may prove loaded in context. Compare these two sentences:

> Jackson is responsible for all the equipment in the office.
> Jackson is responsible for the broken typewriter.

The first sentence simply indicates that Jackson controls all the equipment. In the second sentence, however, the word "responsible" seems to mean that Jackson not only broke the typewriter but will have to pay for it.

Now compare two questions with virtually the same meaning:

> You're really serious about this project, aren't you?
> Are you really serious about this project?

TABLE 2. *A guide to loaded terms in English*

Type of term	Examples (or explanation)
Obscenities	("Four-letter" words referring to sexual or body functions)
Blasphemies	(Expressions containing references to God or Jesus)
Political references	left/right-wing, radical, communist(ic), fascist(ic) reactionary, archconservative
Religious references	(Slang words for religious affiliation, e.g., "Papist" for "Catholic")
Ethnic references	(Slang words for race or nationality, e.g., "Redskin" for "American Indian")
Negative references to others' intelligence	stupid, idiotic, foolish, dumb, silly, illogical, imbecile, moron, dim-witted, obtuse, naive, simple-minded
Negative references to others' character	crooked, dirty, devious, ambitious, aggressive, underhanded, arrogant, sly, immoral, unethical, unprofessional, sinful
Negative references to others' positions	crazy, conspiracy, scheme, plot, fabrication, preposterous, self-serving, ill-conceived, simplistic, wrong/softheaded, outrageous, reckless, ridiculous, unimaginative

The second question implies criticism; it is loaded.

The exercises for this chapter (in Appendix I) provide further opportunity to study loaded words.

Emphasis

Finally, a few remarks on emphasis are necessary. How do writers emphasize the points they consider important? And how, in doing so, do they avoid appearing biased?

Emphasis begins with the writer's choice of subject. Let us assume that an engineer is asked to survey various kinds of steam jets to determine which should be installed in a new factory. Logically, the engineer would write a report comparing them. He or she may find one product clearly superior, however, and devote the entire report to it.

Emphasis is next achieved through careful organization. Here, using the order of importance is helpful; the writer marshals the evidence—that is, arranges the arguments like stepping stones—so that the most important comes last. This process makes possible a smooth transition to the conclusion and recommendations.

Sometimes, of course, ideas need to be emphasized in mid-report. There are two incorrect methods of providing emphasis:

1. *Hyperbole.* Overstatement should be avoided. Words like "fantastic" and "terrible" are not appropriate to professional writing. Even "excellent" is too strong if the correct term is "good."

2. *Exclamation marks.* Emphasis is rarely achieved by using exclamation marks (!). The best policy is to avoid them.

To emphasize something in mid-report, underline a key word, or at most a very important sentence. Depend upon the reader's intelligence to accomplish the rest.

Summary

Professional communications place heavy responsibilities on the writer or speaker, and the pressure sometimes stimulates emotion. It is important, however, to avoid emotion—particularly anger—and to adopt a neutral tone. Our opponents' positions cannot be attacked with offensive language, and our own positions should not be overstated.

Chapter 14

Visual Materials in Reports

English words can only be used by English speakers, but visual information belongs to everyone. Moreover, words are often ineffective vehicles for certain information, which needs to be transmitted by numbers (considered here as part of the universal visual language) or by lines or by pictorial representations. This chapter examines the most common such "visuals."

First, a few words are necessary about the relationship between words and visuals in writing. Many reports, as indicated above, should have visuals, but *all* reports must have words. Visuals, accordingly, are subordinate; they support the text and must be organized logically within the text.

Thus, if a table or diagram is crucial to understanding a major point, it should appear at the place where that point is being discussed; if it is helpful but not crucial, it may be placed at the end of the text. Again, readers should not be delayed. Many will be annoyed if they must break from the text and flip to the end of the report to find an important table or figure.

In Chapter 12, to be sure, it was suggested that an entire appendix might be created to contain technical data such as calculations. Numerous visuals may, in fact, become awkward in a text. If "crucial" visuals are placed in an appendix, however, they should be referred to in the text: for example, "Table 5, in the appendix, demonstrates this inconsistency" or "A diagram of the process has been supplied in the appendix (Fig. 6, p. 33)."

A further point about the relationship of words and visual information is the need to explain visuals. Usually a table or a graph contains only small details, particularly numbers. Few non-technical readers are satisfied with simple numerical statements; they will want the writer to explain the findings in words, even when the evidence in the visual would be clear to the technically trained. To be safe, a good writer not only introduces the visual but summarizes its message. For example:

> Figure 3 graphs the three products' resistance to lateral loading, and demonstrates the superiority of our product for windy terrain.

Sometimes an explanation is written below the figure, in addition to, or instead of, a label.

Finally, visuals should be clear and simple. The major purpose of tables, graphs, charts, diagrams, calculations, and other visuals is to simplify the presentation of complex material. If the visual is badly organized, or overcomplex, this purpose is defeated.

We turn now to specific visuals, their purposes, and the rules governing their use. For convenience, they are divided into tables, linear figures, and representational figures.

Tables

A table is the most common method of expressing a series of facts. Whereas all other visuals are usually numbered and labeled as "figures," tables are *called* tables, and are numbered separately. They are best introduced by looking first at "informal tables."

Informal tables.   Much writing includes lists such as series of numbers, itineraries for a trip, or agendas for meetings:

> 9:30 a.m.—Registration
> 10:00 a.m.—Welcome from the President
> 10:15 a.m.—Keynote speech: "The State of Polymer Research To-
> day"
> etc.

Such simple lists do not constitute tables, however. Usually they are incorporated stylistically into the text; no number or label is assigned.

Formal tables.   By contrast, a formal table is more than a list. It cannot be read simply as part of the text, for it usually contains both a vertical and a horizontal row of headings, both of which control the data. Therefore, the reader must read first one way and then the other. An example is shown in Figure 10.

Table (and figure) numbers and labels may start from the left margin, as in this case, or be centered above the visual. Like all titles, the label should accurately but briefly state the table's contents. The contents themselves must be presented clearly, efficiently, and attractively, which means careful attention to proportions and to white space. If possible, the

TABLE 43

THE GREEN REVOLUTION—POPULATION GROWTH IN COUNTRIES PRIMARILY AFFECTED, 1960–1985
(in millions)

	Population Increase 1960–1969	Population 1970	Estimated Increase 1970–1979	Population 1980	Expected Increase 1970–1985	Population 1985
India	125.6	555.0	170.4	725.0	253	808
Pakistan	44.2	136.9	51.0	187.0	87	224
Indonesia	27.7	121.2	32.3	153.5	63	184
Mexico	14.7	50.7	20.7	71.0	34	85
Philippines	10.7	38.1	17.7	56.0	26	64
Ceylon	2.7	12.6	3.7	16.5	5	18
Total	+225.6	914.5	+295.8	1,210.0	+468	1,383

Source: Calculated by author on the basis of data from United Nations and Population Reference Bureau.

FIG. 10. *Example of a formal table. [From Georg Borgstrom, Focal Points (New York: Macmillan, 1973), p. 298.]*

table should be placed upright on the page, so that the reader does not need to turn the report sideways.

Linear Figures

Tables and calculations contain specific, or direct, data. Other visuals—"figures"—present data indirectly: They show trends, proportions, or graphics which suggest that the readers "see for themselves." Thus, they are numbered consecutively, as a group, even though they may look quite different.

Graphs and charts are the most abstract of this group. They may be termed linear because they use lines to present information.

Graphs. "What are the population growth rates for China, Brazil, and the Soviet Union?" "What are the comparative stress analyses for materials used in quake-proof buildings?" "Which company, A or B, has been making better profits in recent years?" These are questions which can be answered most clearly by the use of graphs.

Graphs are dynamic; they show movement. When the reader wants to see development under changing conditions, and to estimate future changes, he or she is better served by a graph than by a table. Compare the table and figure shown in Figure 11, for example. Obviously, the graph would answer an investor's questions more quickly.

A graph may have a single line or, like that in Figure 11, several, so that it makes comparisons. Too many lines, however, cause confusion— exactly what visuals should *not* do. Label each line either on the graph or in a legend, or key, below the graph. In either case, make the lines

Table 1

Profits, Four Companies
1977–1981
(in millions)

	1977	1978	1979	1980	1981
Company A	118.77	105.45	113.05	125.41	133.01
Company B	281.03	293.75	300.81	298.45	296.1
Company C	183.69	189.97	197.82	200.96	205.67
Company D	210.11	227.29	202.46	208.19	234.93

Figure 1

Profit Growth, Four Companies
1977–1981 (1976 Base)

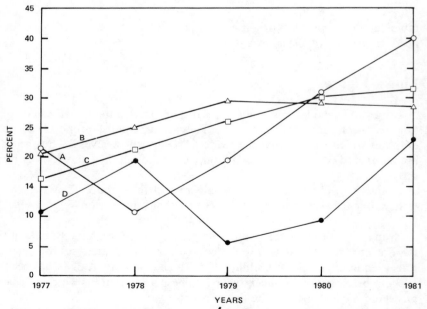

FIG. 11. *Example of the presentation of the same data in the form of a table and a graph.*

different in appearance:

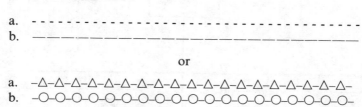

Different colors may also be used, especially in oral presentation.

Numbers and labels may be placed above or below graphs and other figures, but should consistently be in one place or the other.

Charts.   There are several types of visuals known as charts, although some are best called diagrams (see below, "Representational Figures"). Whereas the graph shows changes, usually over time, the chart shows proportions or relationships at a given point in time. The most common of these, in non-technical fields, is the pie chart (also called pie diagram). As the example in Figure 12 demonstrates, the pie chart is the simplest way to show the distribution of a certain "whole" among its parts.

Another non-technical visual is the organization chart, an example of which is shown in Figure 13. Before large, publicly owned companies existed, there was little need for such a chart, which is meant to show the

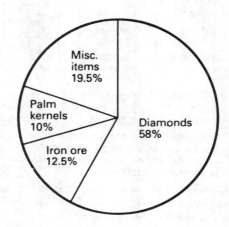

Fig. 2   Sierra Leone: Exports 1968
(£36.2 million)

FIG. 12. *Example of a pie chart. [From N. J. H. Grant and C. R. Wang'ombe, English in Use: Students' Book 2 (London: Longman, 1979), p. 16.]*

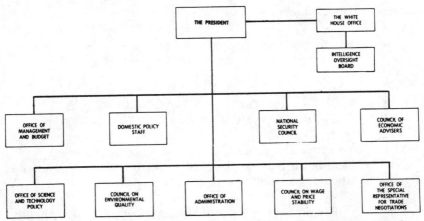

FIG. 13. *Organization chart for the executive office of the United States President.*

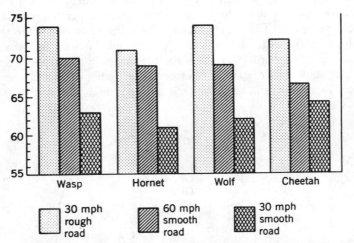

Figure 9. Interior Sound Level in Four Compact Cars (in decibels, A scale). A reading of 50 decibels is comparable to the sound level in a home; 70 decibels is comparable to the sound of a freight train at a distance of 100 feet.

FIG. 14. *Example of a bar chart. [From Theodore A. Sherman and Simon S. Johnson, Modern Technical Writing, 3rd ed., © 1975, p. 129. Reprinted by permission of Prentice-Hall, Inc., Englewood Cliffs, N.J.]*

administrative structure of an organization; today it is often the first company document a management consultant wants to see.

A more useful type for scientists and engineers is the bar chart, which breaks data down into several categories and subcategories, and shows their relative proportions. Note the example in Figure 14, which compares

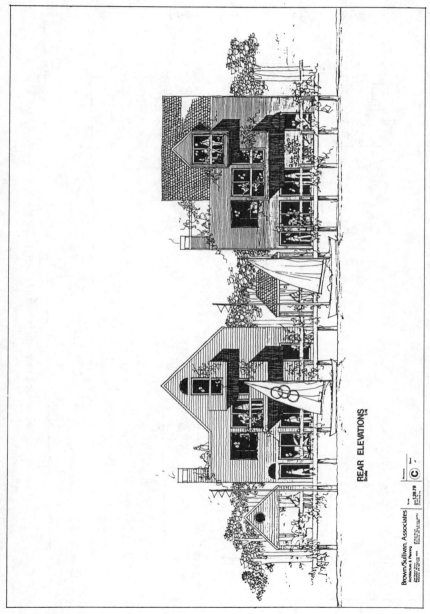

Fig. 15. *Architect's conception of two private residences. [Courtesy of Brown/Sullivan/Arfaa, Architects, Planners.]*

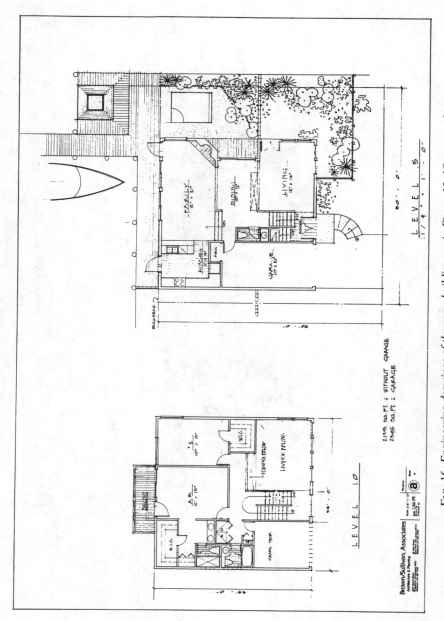

Fig. 16. *Engineering drawings of the same buildings as in Figure 15. [Courtesy of Brown/Sullivan/Arfaa, Architects, Planners.]*

noise levels in four compact cars, but is also able to compare them at different vehicle speeds on different road surfaces.

By this point it should be clear that visuals serve different purposes. Writers must study their data to see which visual will explain the information best, or whether any visual will express that information as simply as sentences and paragraphs.

Representational Figures

Both tables and linear figures are abstract: the former usually rely on absolute numbers, the latter on relative numbers (percentages or trends). The value of such visuals depends upon our ability to analyze abstract information and use it productively.

Certain other visuals are employed to help the reader literally *see* information. For example, when the National Commission on the Causes and Prevention of Violence issued a report on the riots in Cleveland, Ohio, during the summer of 1968, the report included numerous photographs of violent incidents (Louis H. Masotti and Jerome R. Corsi, *Shoot-*

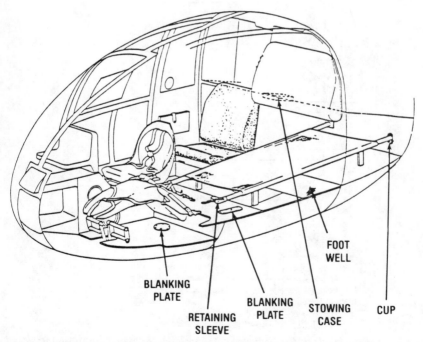

Fig. 17. *Cutaway diagram of a helicopter cabin. Drawing courtesy of Concepts 80, Inc., Newtown Square, Pa.*

Out in Cleveland: Black Militants and the Police, Washington, D.C.:
Government Printing Office, May, 1969). No words could express the
seriousness of the situation so effectively.

Photographs are usually not a practical visual, however. They are

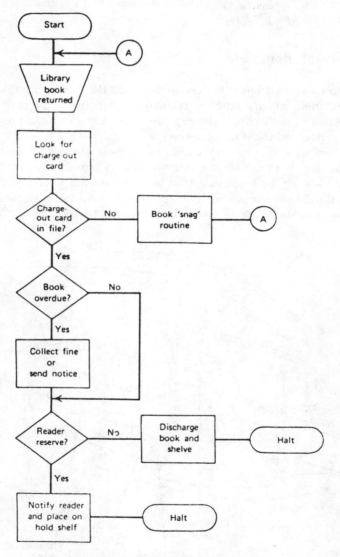

FIGURE 6. *Flow-chart figure: discharge of a library book.*

FIG. 18. *Example of a flow diagram. [From Allen Kent and Harold Lancour, ed.,
The Encyclopedia of Library and Information Science, vol. 8 (New York: Marcel
Dekker, Inc., 1972), p. 573.]*

expensive and require special processing for use in a text. Moreover, some visual information cannot be photographed. An example is the drawing made of a building before it has been built.

Two representations of such a building are shown in Figures 15 and 16. Figure 15 is an architect's drawing, which is meant to give a "feeling" for two private homes—how they will look in their environment, what ideas and pleasant images they will suggest. Figure 16 is an engineer's drawing, which "visualizes" the buildings only in terms of their parts and proportions.

Two other representational figures may serve a report well: the "cutaway" diagram and the flow chart.

Cutaways.   Machinery is often housed in a casing; no one can observe the action of the machine. Thus, a report writer describing the machine might "cut away" the casing in a drawing, so that the reader can see the machine's parts. An example is shown in Figure 17.

A cutaway diagram is especially useful when the purpose of the report is to explain the function of each of the machine's parts. Unfortunately, it requires an artistic ability which most writers lack.

Flow charts.   Flow diagrams (or flow charts) are the correct visual for demonstrating a process. Sometimes they are abstract, as in the economist's diagram of monetary flow, but they are just as likely to be concrete, as in a diagram which shows the flow of blood through the body.

Flow diagrams may use "cutaway" elements; a visual on blood flow would require the writer to "take off" flesh, so that the heart and blood vessels could be seen. Often they can be drawn with a few arrows, however. An example is shown in Figure 18.

Summary

Visual materials aid nonnative writers by reducing complex information to simple forms. The writer must choose the correct visual, the correct place for it in the text, and the correct label for it. Generally, the writer should also "explain" it in the text, or at least indicate why the visual is important enough to be included.

Chapter 15

Papers and Publications

Many professional people are employed in research; many others feel they have knowledge which should be communicated to colleagues. Such people will seek to publish their ideas, or at least to give formal presentations. Thus we come to the highest level of writing in the professions: the article or formal paper.

Publishing an article or presenting a paper is an honor and a privilege. Yet in some ways, it makes life difficult. People who wish to communicate an idea to other experts in their fields have the responsibility of researching carefully, presenting the facts accurately, and—hardest of all—accepting criticism from others. Perhaps the best advice for those who want to publish is this: Ask for criticism; let colleagues comment on the work before it appears in public. Not even a genius can write a perfect paper.

It follows that even a short paper may take weeks of preparation. This chapter considers writing for publication from its earliest stages to the last, which is submitting the manuscript to a journal.

Getting Started

Experts compete with one another, yet they also help one another. Often, young scientists are asked to join a project headed by a senior researcher. If the senior person is generous, he or she includes younger researchers as co-authors of publications resulting from the project. The younger researchers are fortunate, for they will soon learn how to develop and publish their own ideas.

Even without such direction, professionals can get help from their colleagues. Professional societies are one good source of assistance. New members of the society should spend a long time listening to the papers and research ideas presented at the meetings. Eventually, they will understand at least two important things: the characteristics of a good paper, and the theories that currently interest specialists in the field.

Furthermore, these professional exchanges often suggest good topics for research. Ideas that develop from individual work in a laboratory or office may not be as good. Experts help one another by talking to one another, and a good research topic often comes as a response to another researcher's idea.

Generally, the topic chosen should have three qualities. First, it should be of interest to others in the field. Second, it should be narrow; young researchers, especially, must show their expertise by first treating small topics very carefully and thoroughly. Third, it should be original. A researcher's reputation is ruined if he or she claims findings which are actually "borrowed" from someone else.

Having chosen a topic which meets these conditions, the writer should turn again to other people before beginning research—to a colleague with good practical sense, or an expert who can evaluate the worth of the topic quickly. Sometimes writers worry that others will steal their ideas. Such thefts do happen, in the English-speaking professional world as elsewhere, but the risk should be taken. A colleague may point out, for example, that the topic has already been treated, and thus save the writer much wasted effort.

Writers who discuss their ideas openly also find themselves receiving support. Colleagues become interested and helpful. Supervisors may provide typing help (or even time off). A colleague in the public relations office might offer to edit the paper, if the writer has problems with English.

Someone in the organization may also have a good idea as to where and how to present the paper. The best suggestion for the first paper may well be to give it before the local professional society, an audience the writer knows. Publication can come later; as the saying goes, "We must walk before we can run."

Research: The Interview

Where does the professional start, in researching a formal paper? With, again, people. Experts in the field have knowledge that has never been published. Just as helpful, they usually know what *has* been published, and where. Accordingly, the writer may wish to interview an expert, which is a common practice.

The foreign-born professional may feel hesitant about going to well-known experts. These people seem important and very busy, and it is true that one or two may say they have no time for an interview. On the other hand, the expert who is genuinely interested in the communication of ideas will often be happy to give an interview. With a few words, an expert may be able to give direction to the research and save the writer many hours of unnecessary work.

The responsibility of the writer/interviewer is to prepare well for the meeting, to make good use of the time given, and to demonstrate a serious, intelligent understanding of the field. A list of rules for conducting an interview would include these:

1. Write the expert well in advance, in a letter which defines your research project, establishes your credentials, and suggests several dates for a meeting.
2. Read the expert's most recent publications and whatever he or she has written on your subject.
3. Develop a list of questions you would like answered.
4. Arrive promptly for the interview with your questions, a notepad, and pencils; if you wish to use a tape recorder, ask the expert's permission first.
5. Write statements exactly; if you expect to quote the expert, read the statement back to him or her, to be sure it is correct.
6. Be natural; treat an expert as a colleague, not a king.
7. Study the notes immediately after the interview, and write them out more carefully, while the discussion is fresh in your memory.

An interview conducted according to these rules will almost always prove valuable to both parties. In addition, an acquaintanceship with a prominent specialist could have benefits for the researcher's career.

Research: The Literature Review

Publishable research does not depend simply on lonely, intensive work at midnight in the laboratory. All papers and publications require a survey of literature, or at least evidence that the writer knows the literature.

So much has been written on every subject that the modern professional must make use of special searching tools. The needed resources are usually available in a technical or university library. Generally speaking, they can be separated into three categories: the card catalogue, indexing or abstracting services, and computerized data retrieval.

The card catalogue.   Most professional persons have a working knowledge of card catalogues, which are found even in small libraries. The library's entire book and monograph collection is catalogued on 3 × 5 inch cards, in drawers which are available to the user. There will be one card under the author's name, one under the title of the work, and at least one representing the work's subject (see Figure 19). The call number of the book—the key to its location—is written on each card.

For professionals engaged in highly specialized research, the card catalogue is mainly useful when the author or the title of a book is known. The catalogue does not include journal articles. Nor is the subject index likely to yield titles of immediate use—at least, until catalogues are computerized.

On the other hand, a technical library may have a collection of "pathfinders," which are guides to research on narrow topics, usually prepared by people who have done the research. Pathfinders were first developed at the Massachusetts Institute of Technology. Although some exchange has taken place among university libraries, the researcher should be aware that the sources contained in the pathfinder may be limited to the library where it is found; note that call numbers are commonly listed for each reference, as in the card catalogue. Pathfinders also go out of date quickly.

Figure 20 shows the first page of a pathfinder.

Indexing and abstracting services.   Although the card catalogue does not list articles, it (or a special journals list) does give locations for the journals in the collection, from *Advances in Astronomy and Astrophysics* to *Zoological Record*. Special journals serve as indexes to articles in other publications and will probably be the first source checked by the experi-

```
            SCIENCE--PHILOSOPHY.

Q
175         Bronowski, Jacob, 1908-
.B7918          The ascent of man [by] J. Bronowski.
1974        [1st American ed.]  Boston, Little,
            Brown [1974, c1973]
                448 p.  illus.  26 cm.
                Bibliography: p. 440-442.




                1. Science--Philosophy.  2. Science--
            History.  3. Man.  I. Title

PPD                         DXUsc        73-20446
```

FIG. 19. *Example of a subject card from a card catalogue.*

LIBRARY PATHFINDER- DREXEL UNIVERSITY   NONVERBAL COMMUNICATION

SCOPE: Nonverbal communication is the
meaningful transfer of thought or
emotion through means other than
words or speaking.

An introduction to this topic ap-
pears in Argyle, Michael. Bodily
Communication (pp.1-17) (1975)
P 99.5 .A7x 1975   Lower Level

BOOKS dealing with nonverbal communica-
tion are listed in the card catalog.
Look for the subjects:
"Nonverbal Communication"
                (highly relevant)
"Communication--Psychological aspects"
                (also relevant)
"Personal space"--(related)

Frequently mentioned texts include:

Siegman, Aron W. and Feldstein,
Stanley, eds.
Nonverbal Behavior and Communication
(1978)
BF 637.C45N62   Lower Level

Birdwhistell, Roy L.
Kinesics and Context; Essays on Body
Motion Communication (1970)
BF 637.C45B57   Reserve Book Room

Ruesch, J., and Kees, W.
Nonverbal Communication: Notes on
The Visual Perception of Human
Relations (1956)
P 90.R8   Lower Level

Hinde, Robert A., editor
Nonverbal Communication (1972)
BF 637 .C45N65   Lower Level

Darwin, Charles
The Expression of the Emotions in Man
and Animals (1965)
QP 401 .D3 1965   2nd Floor - S/T

Other books on nonverbal communication
are shelved under call numbers
BF 637 .C45   Lower Level

An ENCYCLOPEDIA containing information
on nonverbal communication is:

Sills, David L., editor
International Encyclopedia of the
Social Sciences v. 8 pp. 379-384 (1968)
H40 .A2i5   1st Floor, Ref Gen

BIBLIOGRAPHIES which contain material on
nonverbal communication include:

Mehrabian, Albert
Nonverbal Communication (1972) pp.206-217
(259 refs.)
BF 637 .C45M43   Lower Level

Key, Mary Ritchie
Nonverbal Communication: A Research Guide
and Bibliography (1977) pp. 142-428 (3,000+
refs.)
P 99.5 .K4   Lower Level

JOURNAL ARTICLES and other literature on
nonverbal communication are indexed
primarily in the guides listed. The
quoted subject headings are those in
use since 1970.

Social Sciences Index (1974+ continues
Social Sciences and Humanities Index.
Covers 250+ journals essential to this
discipline.)
See:
"Communication, Nonverbal"
AI 3.S6x   1st Floor,Gen Ref Table

Current Index To Journals In Education
(1969+, covers 700+ publications representing the core periodical literature
in the field of education.)
See:
"Nonverbal Communication"
Z 5813 .C8   1st Floor,Gen Ref Table

Psychological Abstracts (1927+, covers
800+ publications from all fields of
psychology.)
See:
"Nonverbal Communication"
BF 1.P65   1st Floor, Gen Ref Tab!

Social Sciences Citation Index (1972+
covers 2,000+ writings related to all
aspects of the social sciences.)
See:
"Nonverbal Communication"
Z 7163 .S6x   1st Floor, Gen Ref Tal·

RC_1

FIG. 20. *Example of a pathfinder. [Reproduced by permission of M. Rita Costello.]*

enced researcher. Among the most comprehensive are *Applied Sciences and Technology Index, Index Medicus,* and *Business Periodicals Index,* which list titles of recent articles under subject headings.

Citation indexes are also useful, particularly in interdisciplinary research. Three such indexes are published by the Institute for Scientific Information in Philadelphia: *Science Citation Index, Arts and Humanities*

Citation Index, and *Social Sciences Citation Index*. These are usually available in research-oriented libraries.

The researcher begins by looking up a relevant article or book under the first author's name. There, he or she will find references to other authors who have cited this material; these latter authors' articles can then be checked to see if their own work will contribute to the research. Since the *Science Citation Index*, for example, annually indexes more than 1,000 books as well as articles from more than 3,000 journals around the world, the researcher is likely to find relevant materials more quickly there than under various subject heads.

Probably the best source for people engaged in research within a recognized field is the journal devoted to abstracts of recently published articles in the relevant field: *Biological Abstracts*, *Chemical Abstracts*, *Engineering Index*, *Psychological Abstracts*, and so on. The volume of the contents may be very large, but the abstracts will be indexed by subject, for easy reference. The benefit here is that researchers learn enough about the content of the article to decide whether or not to read it.

The "Further Reading" list at the end of this part suggests books which treat indexing and abstracting services in detail.

Information retrieval. Finding data is perhaps harder today than ever before, for at least three reasons: so much is published; so much is *not* published; and so much modern research is interdisciplinary in nature. Research on a new building material, for example, might be published in a civil engineering, a materials engineering, an architecture, or a chemical journal. Similarly, an article on legal problems in the Medicaid program might appear in legal, medical, or government publications.

The researcher will need to look through a citation index and perhaps several abstracting services, but may take even a further step. Once again, people—in this case, reference librarians—are important. In a technical library, a good reference librarian can probably name a dozen journals in several fields (and perhaps a government publication) where data might be found. Increasingly, too, librarians use computers to retrieve information from a central information bank.

In Palo Alto, California, for example, the Lockheed Corporation has an information system ("Dialog") which stores titles of periodical articles from around the world. Librarians with a computer-telephone connection to Dialog can search a huge volume of literature for articles relating to a researcher's topic. Starting with a topic code, they move into a variety of subtopics, and the computer will quickly print the titles, sources, and short descriptive abstracts of the relevant articles.

There is still no way, however, to search all the literature with computers. For one thing, several information systems exist, none of which is comprehensive; they include the Medlars-Medline system of the National

Library of Medicine and the OCLC (the Ohio College Library Consortium) system. Within each information system, moreover, there are often several data banks. In addition, information systems depend on the same abstracting services which the writer may already have reviewed.

One other important point: Information systems may contain only recent publications. For older literature, the writer should consult whatever printed bibliographies exist. In short, traditional, non-electronic research tools continue to be necessary, despite the increasing access by computer to data banks.

Writing the Paper

It is not necessary to finish the research before beginning to write the paper. Indeed, it may be helpful to write out good ideas as they occur, and to assemble a rough draft as the research is being completed. The rule is then to rewrite—and to rewrite again.

The value of the paper depends generally on four criteria: content, organization, style, and appearance. Style includes grammatical use of English; guidance is provided in the Appendices II and III. The other three criteria need some development here, beginning with content.

Content.   Writers must not forget that a published article is a guide to others. If it contains inconsistencies, it causes confusion. If it contains inaccuracies, it is misleading and a disservice to others. The data therefore must be true, and the writer should check them very carefully.

"Data" means facts, not expressions of opinion, particularly in technical fields. Researchers should resist the temptation to make assumptions or to express unsupported beliefs. Rather, they should state proofs—even proof that their original hypotheses were wrong. A disproved hypothesis also deserves to be communicated.

All in all, a rigorous honesty is the first duty of those who deliver papers and write articles for publication. For some, it is also the most difficult duty. They are tempted to change data to make their results impressive. They may even go to the extreme of borrowing others' ideas and data, an act which is considered unprofessional.

The term for this offense is plagiarism; it refers to borrowing either data or language without permission or without acknowledgment. Whenever writers want to use another author's words, they must give that author credit. They may *not* use the other author's data except to support their own independent ideas, and again, acknowledgment is necessary.

Organization.   "Brevity." "Economy." "Tight writing." These are terms used to characterize well-written professional papers. In part, they imply style—usually, the elimination of either repetition or unnecessary adjectives and adverbs. Economy also refers to content; the good writer leaves out irrelevant material, however interesting it may seem. But most of all, tight writing means good organization.

In the broadest terms, a paper identifies a problem and suggests a solution. Along the way, it also devotes space to a survey of literature, a description of the methodology used in research, and a discussion of results. Often, particularly in the sciences, a strict format is expected of the writer. In the biological sciences, for example, this organization is standard:

1. Introduction
2. Materials and Methods
3. Results (data)
4. Discussion (conclusions)

Writers must know the structure expected in journals to which they submit their work.

Within each section, logical development is important. The introduction must state the problem—and its importance—clearly; in some cases, the literature review, the conclusions, and even the methodology used will also appear here. The other sections may be developed by one of the rhetorical modes identified in Chapter 10: a classification of materials, a process mode for methods, and so on.

"Tight organization" is, in fact, a synonym of "tight writing." When we consider that many technical publications prefer articles only two pages long, we realize how important it is to put the pieces carefully into order.

Manuscript conventions.　Appendix II includes a basic guide for the appearance of the paper in its final draft. In all cases, manuscripts must be typed double-spaced on one side only of bond paper. Unfortunately, many variations exist in other respects.

There are many business journals, for example, but no one set of manuscript conventions for business writers. The style manual for the biological sciences sets widely accepted manuscript conventions, yet some journals in that field have individual variations. The format for equations in a mathematics journal may be unacceptable in a physics journal. And so on.

This does not mean that a carefully typed manuscript will be rejected simply because it does not meet the journal's conventions. It does suggest that the writer consider the journal he or she wishes to publish in before typing the final copy. Editors react in a human—that is, friendly—way to manuscripts which show that the writer has taken the time to make their job easier.

Submitting the Manuscript

Clearly, choosing a journal is a process which begins before the writing is complete. But how does one choose? First, of course, by elimination. Journals which have not dealt with the general subject covered by the article will not be interested; their editors—and reviewers—may fail to see the importance of the research.

Next, the writer eliminates journals which are either "lightweight" or "heavyweight" in the importance of their contents. Perhaps a first article, or one which the writer recognizes as minor, should be sent to the former type. More often, writers believe in the importance of their work and choose a "heavyweight" journal.

At this point there should be three or four journals left. The final selection may be made on the basis of circulation—that is, by determining which is the most widely read. Usually journals declare their circulation (reader subscriptions) in their November or December issues. An even better guide may be *Journal Citation Reports*, published annually by the Institute for Scientific Information; here, in a few minutes, one can discover which journal is read most seriously by other authors.

The journal having been chosen, it is time to look closely at the correct manuscript conventions, which the journal will publish under (usually) the title "Instructions to Authors." The writer should also take the trouble to read a recent issue, looking simply at stylistic matters: headings, footnotes, equations, etc. In the preparation of the manuscript, the writer tries to think like the copy editor who will prepare the article for publication.

The final step in preparation is proofreading (careful reading of the typed manuscript). Many writers trust their typists too much, with the result that they send off manuscripts containing embarrassing errors. The final copy should be read aloud, preferably with another person listening and reading a separate copy.

The original and one copy are sent to the journal in a strong manila envelope. Because editors receive many manuscripts, they will want a covering letter—something which tells them whether the submission is new or a revision, for example. They may also require return postage (by first-class mail).

The writer now waits, probably a long time, for a response. The serious journals will have the manuscript reviewed, and reviewers are not always prompt. Besides, there are other manuscripts on the editor's mind. Indeed, even an accepted article cannot always be scheduled for production in the near future.

What are the chances of a first paper being accepted? Not good. After all the work, and the long wait, the writer may find that the article is rejected. Possibly, however, it will receive a "conditional" acceptance, which means that the editor wants corrections but would like to publish the article. A conditional acceptance may well be considered success.

A rejection is not failure, however. Another journal may like the article. Even if it is not published, it may make a good conference paper. Above all, a rejection accompanied by the editor's and reviewers' criticisms will help the writer construct a better article next time.

Summary

Publication is the final test of professionalism—the measure of the professional's knowledge, reliability, and achievement. Those who wish to publish must be willing to accept long hours of work, criticism, delayed recognition, and often disappointment. These hardships are necessary, however; they train the writer in the high standards of research and scholarship.

Further Reading

(Note: For specialized handbooks, see the "Further Reading" list at the end of Appendix II.)

Andrews, Deborah C., and Margaret D. Blickle. *Technical Writing: Principles and Forms.* New York: Macmillan, 1978

Coleman, Peter, and Ken Brambleby. *The Technologist as Writer.* New York: McGraw-Hill, 1969

Cremmins, Edward T. *The Art of Abstracting.* Philadelphia: ISI Press, 1982

Day, Robert A. *How to Write and Publish a Scientific Paper.* Philadelphia: ISI Press, 1979

Dodds, Robert H. *Writing for Technical and Business Magazines.* New York: John Wiley and Sons, 1969

Engel, S. Morris. *Analyzing Informal Fallacies.* Englewood Cliffs, N.J.: Prentice-Hall, 1980

Estrin, Herman A. "Writing for Publication." *Journal of Technical Writing and Communication*, V. no. 2 (1975), pp. 99–102

Mathes, J. C., and Dwight W. Stevenson. *Designing Technical Reports: Writing for Audiences in Organizations.* Indianapolis: Bobbs-Merrill, 1976

Mitchell, John H. *Writing for Professional and Technical Journals.* New York: John Wiley and Sons, 1968

Rescher, Nicholas. *Introduction to Logic.* New York: St. Martin's Press, 1964

Sherman, Theodore A., and Simon S. Johnson. *Modern Technical Writing.* Englewood Cliffs: Prentice-Hall, 1975

Appendix I

Exercises for Chapters 2 to 15

Exercises for Chapter 2 (pp. 9–17)

1. Assume that you are about to be interviewed for a very desirable job. What nonverbal strategy would you use to make a good impression?

2. Discuss appropriate behavior in the following situations:

a. You have overslept. You have just enough time to get to an important meeting, but you haven't shaved (or, if a woman, you haven't brushed your hair).

b. You are early for a large meeting. Two other people are there before you. They are seated across from each other in the middle of a long table. Where do you sit?

c. The boss calls you to his office, and accuses you, angrily, of a mistake you didn't make.

d. You meet an important professional at the end of a party. You need to talk with this person but the hostess has just made a last offer of coffee.

e. Your colleagues decide to have lunch together to continue discussion of a problem which you are working on too. They seem to forget to invite you.

3. Examine the picture in Figure A1 on the next page. Assume that the man, a salesman, is trying to persuade the woman to hire him. Now discuss these questions:

a. What is the woman's reaction to the man? How do you know?

b. What is your own reaction to the man? Why?

Exercises for Chapter 3 (pp. 18–23)

1. The following are brief glimpses of speakers making mistakes in nonverbal communication while speaking to American audiences. What are the mistakes, and why?

a. A permanent resident in the United States is asked to explain the difficulties of the immigration process to a group of social workers. He appears in the flowing robes of his native country.

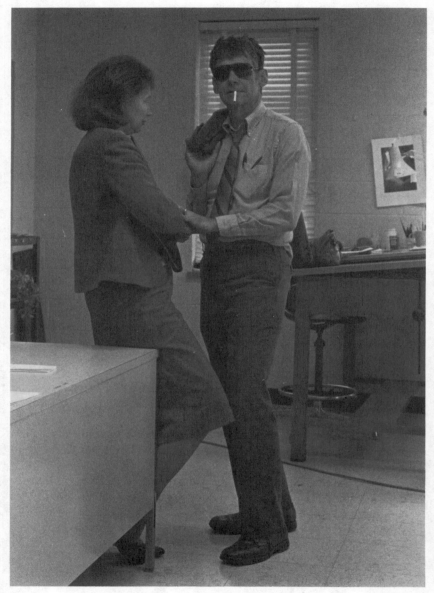

FIG. A1. *Illustration for problem 3, Chapter 2.*

b. While sitting on a stage, waiting to be introduced, the speaker combs her hair.

c. A woman 5 feet 1 inch tall speaks from behind a podium 4 ft 6 inches high.

d. An engineer turns to a blackboard to draw a diagram, and draws it without speaking.

e. A speaker pauses to run his tongue over his lips because they feel dry.

f. A spokesman for the power industry is trying to persuade his audience to support nuclear energy. He gestures by lifting his fingers from the sides of the podium while keeping his thumbs flat on the podium.

g. A man unbuttons his suitcoat as he rises to make his speech.

h. As he is being introduced, the speaker walks toward the podium. Before the woman introducing him has finished, he is standing beside her.

i. The commencement speaker at a large university steps from behind the podium and puts his elbow on it.

j. Asked to give a short presentation of his company's services, a marketing manager pulls 15 pages of paper from his pocket in full view of his audience.

k. A speaker is recommending a paperback book to his audience. As he speaks, he squeezes and twists the book in his hands.

l. Seeing someone in the audience who is not paying attention, the speaker glares at that person throughout his talk.

2. Standing before a mirror, use your hands (a) to make an important point; (b) to raise a rhetorical question; (c) to raise a real question—one you can't answer; (d) to dismiss an idea; (e) to emphasize a word; (f) to show divisions in opinions or data (e.g., "on the one hand" and "on the other hand"). Practice these gestures until they feel natural.

3. Stephen Price, in an article listed under "Further Reading" at the end of Part I, writes that vowels are easy to say, "but we get power and clarity into our speech with consonants." He recommends saying this sentence aloud several times, for practice: "Leaves, frost crisped, break from the trees and fall." Price and others also recommend these exercises for pronouncing words more clearly:

a. Repeat the alphabet several times in front of a mirror.

b. Whistle your favorite songs for 5 minutes a day.

c. Force air out of your diaphragm several times, by placing your hands just under your chest and pushing. Then repeat a long sentence in one breath, pushing on your diaphragm the same way.

d. Repeat a poem of four lines in one breath, taking care to pronounce the last word in each line clearly; breathe from the diaphragm.

Exercises for Chapter 4 (pp. 24–29)

1. Audiovisual aids used in a presentation should be limited to "one or two types." Cite at least two reasons why this is so.

2. A chalkboard is an excellent aid in teaching, and can be useful in presentations too, but it causes several problems. Draw up a list of rules for the correct use of a chalkboard.

3. Draw a rectangle, and consider it an empty room. You are to "fill" it with furniture and aids for a presentation. Begin by considering a presentation you could give—or have given—to an audience of 50 to 100 people. What would be the ideal room design for such a presentation? In designing the room (including seating arrangements for the audience), assume that you will use a flip chart and one type of electronic media, and also that you will distribute reproduced materials. In all of this, consider the location of the doors.

Exercises for Chapter 5 (pp. 33–37)

1. Without reviewing the chapter, answer the following questions:
   a. Very generally, what is the best way to read successfully?
   b. Name four causes of slow reading.
   c. When should the reader stop reading to look up vocabulary items?
   d. What is the difference between "understanding" and "retaining"?
   e. What is the three-step process for good retention?
   f. Define "skimming" and state at least three things readers look for when they skim.
   g. What is the message given by Figure 4 (p. 36)?
   h. Define "recitation."
A good reader could have read the chapter in 5 minutes. How long did it take you? Why?

2. Write a one-paragraph summary of the chapter, from memory.

3. Find a short article in your field which you have not read, and skim it in a few seconds. Then generate questions which you think the article will answer. Next, read the article, and see if it answered your questions. If not, was it the writer's fault, or your fault? Why?

4. Think of an article or a memo which you read two weeks ago but did not re-read or study. From memory, make a list of its major points. Then review it; how much had you forgotten?

Exercises for Chapter 6 (pp. 38–44)

1. Table 1 (p. 43) contains most of the discourse markers used in English. Here are eight which might be added to the list:

indeed	in comparison
otherwise	even so
as an illustration	accordingly
previously	to be specific

Place these terms in the correct "Notional Category" on the table.

2. Review the first passage from *The Affluent Society*, and identify discourse markers. Where there are no obvious discourse markers connecting ideas, what words make the connections?

3. Find the topic sentences in the second passage from *The Affluent Society*. Why is it difficult to identify topic sentences in paragraphs 2 and 3?

4. List all the items in Chapter 6—headings, discourse markers, etc.—that a reader should notice in skimming.

Exercises for Chapter 7 (pp. 45–50)

1. Reverse the models in the chapter: *Mark* the first passage from *The Closing Circle*; and *write marginalia* beside the second or third passage.

2. Without reviewing the passage, try to answer these questions about Commoner's discussion of phosphate:

   a. About how rapidly has phosphate output increased since 1910?

   b. What other pollutants have increased in output? Name three.

   c. Name several pollutants which were unknown before World War II.

3. Review the third passage from *The Closing Circle*. Where are the topic sentences of the three paragraphs?

Exercises for Chapter 8 (pp. 51–56)

1. A test reading passage follows, drawn from Borgstrom's *Focal Points*, pp. 99–100. There are 283 words in the passage, excluding the heading. Skim it in 10 seconds, and spend 10 to 15 seconds generating two or three questions you expect it to answer. Before begining to read, note the time exactly. The instant you finish, note it again.

Limitations in Sight

Let us return to the prairie provinces. Over the past twenty-five years there is hardly a region in North America that has bestowed more care upon its water and soils. Only in very limited areas is the annual precipitation sufficient to allow for average wheat yields. Winter wheat simply cannot be grown there and, as in vast sections of the Soviet Union, Canada has been forced to resort to spring wheat. But in normal years only the southern part of the prairie provinces receives the 12 inches required for a reasonable yield. Dry autumns inevitably bring about lower yields the following year.

The most striking feature of grain cultivation in these regions is therefore the big fluctuation in acre-yields between years. In 1962 the acre-yield for wheat, for instance, was almost twice that of the previous year, and, in 1966, two and a half times as big. In 1967 it was 29 per cent lower than in 1966. Despite all advances in technology and genetics, man is constantly reminded of the harsh restrictions of the northern latitudes for crop production.

To all the complications plaguing Canadian agriculture should be added unreliable harvesting weather. Unfortunately, the month of September is often rainy, even snow sometimes falls. This happened in the fall of 1965 and delayed harvesting for two to three weeks, thus impairing the quality of the grain and reducing the value of the wheat harvest by $100 million. In volume it was a bumper crop, which in turn diminished the protein content. In addition, transportation and storage facilities were inadequate and became bottlenecks hindering grain deliveries. Thus fluctuations in acre-yields cause troublesome disturbances, not the least in such "good" years.

Record your time. You are reading with acceptable speed if you finished the passage in less than 1 minute.

2. The following is a paraphrase, or restatement, of the ideas in the reading passage. Key words have been omitted. Fill in the blank spaces *without reviewing the passage above.*

> The author writes of the _____ provinces in _____.
> The major crop is _____, but yields are often low due to too little _____. This area cannot grow _____ wheat, and only in the _____ parts of the provinces is there a reasonable yield of _____ wheat—and then, only when the previous _____ is wet.
> Annual yields therefore _____ widely. The 1962 crop was almost _____ as large as the _____ crop. Another good year was _____. In brief, _____ latitudes do not produce predictable crops.
> The weather is particularly _____ at harvesting season—for example, the month of _____. In 1965, a delay in harvesting caused by _____ reduced the value of the wheat crop by $_____ million. The fact that it was a _____ crop meant not only that it contained less _____, but that _____ and _____ facilities were inadequate.

It is expected that the blanks requiring dates and amounts will be difficult to answer, but those asking for general information—e.g., paragraph 1—can be completed by a good reader.

3. Now reread the passage, and mark it as follows: underlining for key words or topic sentences only; straight margin lines beside important sentences; brackets beside key details or transitional sentences.

4. Capture the core ideas via one of the modes of reduction. Try not to exceed 100 words.

Exercises for Chapter 9 (pp. 61–64)

1. Read each sentence below. At the end of the sentence is a blank space to enter "I" if the sentence would be found in the introduction of a paper; "B" if it would be found in the body; and "C" if it would be found in the conclusion.

    a. Clearly the machine should be bought immediately. _____

    b. Four principal causes of metal fatigue must be identified. _____

    c. To summarize, here are the major findings. _____

    d. The second effect of better lighting will be increased productivity. _____

    e. First, set the 30°–60° triangle on the T-square. _____

    f. On the other hand, it would be good public relations to give the order to a local supplier. _____

    g. It is important that we consider the proposed merger carefully. _____

    h. Perhaps, then, this is not the best company in the world—but no other is trying harder. _____

    i. (3) *Loss.* When a sound is not easily produced or heard in its environment, it usually disappears. _____

    j. Mr. Harold Smith of Chicago has been appointed Executive Director of the Leonard Museum, effective March 23. _____

    k. The costs of the three items were 12¢, 8¢, and 5¢, respectively. _____

    l. From the confusion of all the arguments pro and con, one point has emerged clearly. _____

    m. The first example of Mr. Jones's incompetence was his failure to service the company limousine. _____

    n. A description follows. _____

    o. It is important to trace the events leading up to the strike. _____

    p. As an Englishman once said, "A penny saved is a penny earned." _____

    q. Turning to the Company B machine, we find similar problems. _____

    r. In view of the problem as outlined above, two recommendations may be made. _____

    s. What is a word-processor, and how does it work? _____

    t. A second type of policy insures the owner against bodily harm to outside contractors. _____

2. Assume that the following is the introduction to a report written by an engineering manager to explain cost overruns on three design projects. You should be able to find several faults.

I didn't approve all the expenses on the Smith design, but left them to John Fry. One day I had a talk with the research group about the amounts they were spending on computer graphing. When I looked at the time sheet, I also found technicians' overtime that didn't seem justified. I immediately made a report, which will be in your files.

Now write an appropriate first sentence for the introduction.

3. Convert the following "part" of an outline into a paragraph on Chicago, to be included in an article about American cities; assume that it follows a paragraph on New York.

    III. Chicago (2nd largest U.S. city): transportation center
        A. O'Hare world's busiest airport
        B. Railroads (Penn Central, Burlington) connect East with northwestern states
        C. Lake Michigan port
          1. St. Lawrence Seaway
          2. Canals connect to Mississippi

Exercises for Chapter 10 (pp. 65–73)

1. Below are topics which might be assigned as writing projects. In the blank space beside each one, state which of the rhetorical modes is suggested by the topic—e.g., pro and con, persuasion, etc. Note that the modes of reduction are excluded from this exercise.

    a. Whether to invest in General Motors, Ford, or Chrysler
    _____

    b. Why American Motors is prospering _____
    c. The debate on smoking in public places _____
    d. How to build a bookshelf _____
    e. How to get to Center City from the plant _____
    f. Why the new steam jet should be bought _____
    g. The good and bad points of opening a branch office in Canada
    _____

    h. How John D. Rockefeller became rich _____
    i. Varieties of primer-sealers _____
    j. What the mail sorter looks like _____
    k. Looking beyond the merger _____
    l. Why the company should hire my son _____
    m. Calculating standard deviations _____
    n. A design for the computer center _____
    o. Two possible lathes for the machine shop _____

2. Consider any large or complicated object—perhaps a machine or a building—and construct two outlines for a description of it. Organize the first outline *spatially*; and organize the second as a classification of its parts or functions.

3. Compare two cities you know well, one in your home country and one elsewhere. Construct whole-to-whole, part-to-part, and likeness-difference outlines; then determine which would lead to a more interesting composition (and if possible, *why*).

Exercises for Chapter 11 (pp. 74–77)

1. Below is a list of possible causes of the economic recession in the United States during the 1980's. Place these causes into order, from most important to least important.

   a. Overspending during the Vietnam War

   b. Detroit's failure to convert to small cars

   c. American dependence on foreign oil

   d. Inefficient labor

   e. The Japanese industrial revolution

   f. Government mismanagement

   g. America's aging industrial plant

   h. Corporate greed

Now write a paragraph logically connecting the last three (f, g, h) in *your* order. Next, try to join the previous two (d, e) in your order.

2. Classify the eight causes of the recession, listed in question 1, into four categories, then into three categories, and then into two.

3. Figure A2 is a drawing of the grounds and plant of a small industry. Below are eight possible outlines for a report describing the plant. *All eight* outlines contain logical flaws. The first one is used as an example, to help you with the other seven.

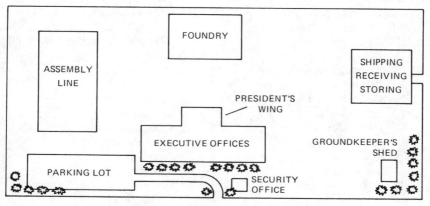

Fig. A2. *Illustration for problem 3, Chapter 11.*

You may occasionally find more than one flaw in an outline.

Outline 1:
    I. Introduction
    II. Executive offices
    III. Shipping, receiving, storing
    IV. Foundry
    V. Other parts of grounds and plant
    VI. Conclusion

Problem: The assembly line is a very important part of the plant. It can't be left out or merely discussed under "Other Parts."

Rule: Be complete; do not omit important topics.

Before working on the problems of the seven outlines which follow, study the drawing in Figure A2. Note its natural divisions, its major and minor parts, and the route you would follow if you were a tour guide for the company. These will help you find the logical flaw in each outline quickly.

After identifying the problem, formulate a rule for good organization, as in the example (Outline 1).

Outline 2:
    I. Introduction
    II. Executive offices and assembly line
    III. Foundry
    IV. Shipping, receiving, storing
    V. Others
    VI. Conclusion

Outline 3:
    I. Introduction
    II. Executive offices
    III. Assembly line
    IV. Foundry
    V. Shipping, receiving, storing
    VI. Parking lot
    VII. Groundskeeper's shed
    VIII. Security office
    IX. Conclusion

Outline 4:
    I. Introduction
    II. Executive offices
    III. Assembly line
    IV. Company products
    V. Foundry
    VI. Shipping, receiving, storing
    VII. Service areas
    VIII. Conclusion

Outline 5:
    I. Introduction
    II. Executive offices
    III. President's wing
    IV. Assembly line
    V. Foundry
    VI. Shipping, receiving, storing
    VII. Service areas
    VIII. Conclusion

Outline 6:
    I. Introduction
    II. Service areas
    III. Executive offices
    IV. Assembly line
    V. Foundry
    VI. Shipping, receiving, storing
    VII. Conclusion

Outline 7:
- I. Introduction
- II. Foundry
- III. Executive offices
- IV. Assembly line
- V. Shipping, receiving, storing
- VI. Service areas
- VII. Conclusion

Outline 8:
- I. Introduction
- II. Executive offices
- III. Assembly line
- IV. Service areas
- V. Foundry
- VI. Shipping, receiving, storing
- VII. Conclusion

Exercises for Chapter 12 (pp. 81–88)

1. The following letter is a letter of transmittal, accompanying a report. It is grammatically correct but has several major flaws. Analyze the letter and suggest corrections.

LAMB ASSOCIATES
Consulting Engineers

3/10/82

Dale Broom
Field's Pipe and Tubing Co.
8000 Old Princeton Road
Haddonfield, N.J.

Dear Dale:

On Feb. 9 I flew to Binghamton. The trip was uneventful, and Rod D'amico met me at the airport, as planned. I stayed at the Valley Inn for three nights, and spent four days observing the recycling cutters in the Allen & Sons plant. That Friday evening I flew back, landing in Philadelphia at 9:32 p.m.
On the basis of this trip I have completed my report on the question of vertical vs. horizontal cutters for Field's Pipette Division, and enclose it. The Allen & Sons people were really helpful. Rod made sure I had access to everything. Their production engineer, Bill Franklin, was also ready to answer any question. The foundry manager, whose name is DeGeer (I think), was equally helpful. The only problem turned out to be my own secretary, who got pneumonia and left me stranded for a month. I had to use a temporary replacement to get the report typed, and you'll have to excuse the mistakes. I caught one large error in the table on standard item cost, but those figures are just educated guesses anyway.

Please let me know if I can be of further help. Although one or two of your people in the Scientific Division have been difficult to work with, we cherish our association with Field's.

$\mathcal{BL}$

Benjamin Lamb, P.E.
President

2. Economy is a good quality in all writing, but especially so in memoranda. Here is a memo which is too wordy; rewrite it to make it shorter, and better.

MEMORANDUM

From: John Francis, Sales Manager
To: Bill Jacobs, Warehouse Supervisor (or staff)
Subj.: Late Delivery of Promised Tables to the Watson Brothers
     Company in Chicago

Mr. Rex Cimorelli, a purchasing agent at the Watson Brothers Company plant in Chicago, Illinois, called me yesterday to report that an order of tables placed six months ago (in January) has not been fulfilled. The order was for fifteen (15) eighteen by forty inch steel-banded work tables (Model TO35UU). I checked with Keith Schnittker, my salesman, who says three months' delivery time is normal. The sales documents also say "Delivery within 90 days."

When I called your office, Jack Soucie, your assistant, said he couldn't trace the shipment. This is bad customer relations. Would you be so kind as to track these tables down and facilitate delivery as soon as possible?

3. Review a report you have written, or one you know well, which does not begin with an executive summary or an abstract. Then write an abstract for it, in non-technical language. As you work, consider the organization of the report: Is it confused, or does it move forward in a straight line?

Exercises for Chapter 13 (pp. 89–94)

1. None of the words in Table 2 (p. 93) will be found in the following sentences. Nevertheless, each sentence contains a loaded word or phrase. Identify these terms, and state the reasons they might offend a reader or an audience.

a. The design team might be laughed at for submitting a proposal which was previously rejected.
b. The idea, irrelevant though it is, appears to be lifted from Watkin's article.
c. The lawyer neglected to do his homework, and disappointed his client.
d. The specifications are as cluttered as a lady's purse.
e. The company will collapse because of its old-fashioned business methods.
f. The manager's thoughts on the matter have been confused.
g. If the technicians will take the time to read their instructions carefully, they will make fewer mistakes.
h. It is time to think seriously about the proposal, however weak you found it.
i. Perhaps Kelly's Irish temperament will prove more dangerous in that situation.
j. Although Kim is only an hourly employee, he has potential in management.

2. Pick out words from the following lists which are too hyperbolic (exaggerated) for use in most professional writing:

> superior, exceptional, magnificent, extraordinary, fabulous, unique, terrific, outstanding, excellent, fantastic, phenomenal, superb
> terrible, weak, poor, awful, unsatisfactory, disgusting, impossible, horrible, bad, inferior, disgraceful, substandard

3. The following Americanisms are heard often in the workplace, but they are too informal for professional writing. Find professional equivalents for them. The first is given as an example.

> The thing went kerplunk/kerpflui/kaput. (The machine or instrument stopped working.)

great	nitty-gritty
okay	beats me
so-so	kind of neat
lousy	couldn't hack it
a snow job	give it the once-over
a bang-up job	messed up the works
a nifty little job	from the word "go"

4. Rewrite the following sentences to give them a more objective tone:
  a. It seems to me Crandall's report is trying to lay the blame for the breakdown on my team.

b. I wish we had more data for making our judgment, but frankly, we did look at all the data available.

c. Your ideas are truly excellent, and we have absolutely no hesitation about following every one of your very perceptive suggestions.

d. You will agree with this finding when you have seen all the facts.

e. The proposed technique is the only solution whatsoever to the problem; the others should be disregarded.

Note: In each case, the correction should be shorter than the original sentence.

Exercises for Chapter 14 (pp. 95–105)

1. The reader should practice constructing tables and linear figures by using data from his or her own professional work. Meanwhile, here is a simple exercise: Convert the absolute numbers in the table below (from Georg Borgstrom, *Focal Points*, New York: Macmillan, 1973) to percentage growth (or decline), on a graph; use the first column as the base (100%). Be sure to follow all manuscript conventions.

2. Design a flow chart for a process you know from your work or research. Construct it so that it will fit vertically on an 8½ × 11 inch piece of paper and so that all points in the process are clearly labeled.

3. Glance through a professional article you have not read, and find a non-representational visual (a table, a graph, or a chart). Then, without reading the article, try to write a paragraph stating the point made by the visual. Next, read the article to see if you were correct. If so, the writer has done his or her job well. But as a final step, compare your paragraph with the visual to see if the writer could have conveyed the information better in words.

TABLE 34

CATTLE STOCK IN SELECTED COUNTRIES, 1948–1970
(in million heads)

	1948–1952*	1961–1965*	1966	1967	1968	1969	1970
1. United States	80.6	103.8	108.9	108.6	109.2	109.9	112.3
2. Brazil	51.3	78.6	90.5	90.0	90.0	92.3	95.0
3. Argentina	42.3	43.1	48.8	51.2	51.5	48.3	48.0
4. Mexico	13.0	20.7	22.4	22.8	23.3	23.6	24.9

.
.
.

* Annual averages.

Exercises for Chapter 15 (pp. 106–115)

1. Construct a pathfinder for research on your special professional interest, for the library you use. Be sure to include call numbers for each source.

2. Compile a list of journals which might be interested in your research, and then evaluate them by the criteria of (a) weightiness, (b) circulation, and (c) citations.

3. Identify a specialist in your field whom you would like to interview, and design the questions you would ask. Then—if you are serious about publishing—request the interview.

4. Look up, in a citation index, an article which interested you; it should be something printed at least two years ago. Then make two judgments: first, whether it interested others as much as it did you; and second, whether it interested others for good or bad reasons (i.e., is it seen as a contribution or a mistake?). Before deciding, review at least four works which cite it.

Appendix II

Mechanics

The term "mechanics" is used here to mean three special considerations in writing which are mechanical in nature: (1) Manuscript Conventions, (2) Spelling, and (3) Punctuation. Basic rules are presented for correct usage, and in each case exercises are provided as aids to better understanding.

A "Further Reading" list of reference works appears at the end of this appendix. It includes handbooks for authors in the sciences, mathematics, medicine, and government, but not in business or engineering, for which no standard handbooks are in use.

Section 1.   Manuscript Conventions

Manuscript conventions are the rules which govern the appearance of a piece of professional writing. They are necessary to prevent confusion or delay on the reader's part.

Manuscript conventions vary by type of writing (letter or report), by organization (government or private company), by learned journal, and by discipline. The following general guidelines for reports and papers can be used in the absence of established conventions. Secretaries may know these conventions well; the writer, however, must retain overall responsibility for the appearance of the work.

Materials

Professional writing of any importance should be typed, not handwritten. Use a modern typewriter with a carbon ribbon (or one which, at least, still gives dark print). A silk ribbon is preferred to a cotton ribbon.

The final manuscript should be typed on 8½ by 11 inch white bond paper. Neither colored paper nor the thin paper known as "onionskin," formerly used for copies, is acceptable. Lined paper should not be used, not even for visuals.

Pagination

Pages are numbered consecutively. The first page, containing the title, is sometimes not numbered, or is numbered at the bottom. It is easier for both reader and typist if succeeding pages are numbered at top-center or top-right.

Titles

As the first message the reader looks for, the title must be displayed prominently. A separate title page may be placed at the beginning of a long piece of writing, containing title, author, and other pertinent information. The title—but not the author's name—then appears again above the text.

The title should be placed one-third, or at least one-fourth, the way down the first page, and centered exactly. If the text is double-spaced, the space between title and text should be triple-spaced. The title may be written entirely in capital letters, or in lower case, with only the first word and other important words beginning with capital letters. It should not be underlined or placed in quotation marks (unless it *is* a quote).

The content of the title must reflect the content of the text, but in as few words as possible. Articles (*a/an/the*) and verbs are often omitted to save space. Sometimes phrases are rearranged for the same purpose, but meaning may become confused. Note this title:

Study of Fish Breeding Habits Banned by Mayor

Was it the study or the breeding habits which were banned?

Headings

Headings have the properties of titles, with three exceptions. First, they should always be short. Second, they may be placed in the center of the page or at the left-hand margin, but consistently in one place or the other. Finally, they may be used to describe function ("Results," "Discussion," etc.) rather than content.

Margins

White space, which rests the reader's eyes and provides space for editing, is to be left on all sides of the text. Leave 1½ inches at the top (excluding the first page) and left side, and at least 1 inch at the right side and bottom. Too little space on the left-hand side prevents the reader from placing the composition in a notebook, and too little space on the right prevents the reader from making notes. Keep the right-hand margin as even as possible, all lines ending within five to seven type-spaces of one another.

The bottom margin should not be raised, except to keep the first line of a new paragraph, or a heading, from being placed on the bottom line. Otherwise, a large amount of white space at the bottom looks like a signal to the reader that the composition has ended.

Paragraphing

As the form for a single idea, the paragraph needs to be separated from its sister paragraphs. The usual method is to indent 5 to 10 type-spaces on a new line; this gives the reader both restful white space and a signal of a new idea. Block paragraphing—starting the paragraph on a new line, at the left-hand margin—offers neither benefit but is required by some organizations. Whichever choice is made should be used consistently.

The right-hand margin should be kept even until the paragraph is finished. Inexperienced writers sometimes avoid starting a new sentence in the last line of the page, thus leaving a large white blank which seems to signal the end of the paragraph. When the new sentence begins at the left-hand margin on the next page, the reader is confused.

Finally, consider paragraph length. Only highly educated readers can manage very long paragraphs (up to a full double-spaced page). Most readers want more frequent breaks; often, long paragraphs can and should be divided, to give a clearer message. On the other hand, a one-sentence paragraph is a contradiction: The correct English paragraph is an idea stated generally and then supported with details. Ideally, paragraphs contain three to eight sentences.

Revisions

Few pieces of writing are well done on the first try. Expect to make a "draft"—a first attempt which will not be the final version—and to make all revisions there. Only when the draft seems exactly right is the final copy to be typed. If numerous errors are made in typing, the composition (or at least some pages) should be retyped.

Occasional small revisions may be made on the final copy, as follows:

1. *Corrections.*   A typing error or spelling mistake should not be erased; this only damages the paper. The wrong letter or word should be covered with a "white-out" product, and the correction should be typed in its place.

2. *Deletions.*   Where a sentence or clause needs to be removed, the entire page should be retyped. One or two words may be deleted, however. Again, the error should be covered with a white substance, not crossed out or erased.

3. *Insertions.*   An omitted word cannot be inserted in a single-spaced document, but may be inserted when the composition is double-spaced. Americans are not accustomed to the British convention of placing a word in the right-hand margin when it is meant for insertion in the middle of the line:

usually

Mark's test scores have/been above the 90th percentile.   /

Instead, place it exactly above the slot where it belongs:

usually
Mark's test scores have/been above the 90th percentile.

A small, handwritten caret (∧) occasionally replaces the slash mark, but is even more noticeable, and less desirable.

Proofreading

At every stage of writing—draft, typed copy, retyped final version—read for errors. Many writers spend hours preparing a composition but fail to spend a few minutes proofreading. The result may be the reader's suspicion that the writer is not really serious about the ideas he or she is presenting.

One effective way to proofread is to read the composition aloud. An English-speaking colleague may also be willing to read for errors. Do not tolerate either errors or messiness. A neat, careful presentation is always appreciated by readers.

Exercises

1. Rewrite the awkward title, "Study of Fish Breeding Habits Banned by Mayor," so that it is clear.

2. Below are two titles for the same project. One is too long, and the other is too short. Combine them into an appropriate title.

   a. The Effects of Red Dye #4 on Laboratory Rats in Experiments Conducted at the University of California/Los Angeles During 1979

   b. Red Dye #4

3. Condense the following sentence into a title which is accurate but as short as possible: The Department of Defense has conducted a study which concludes that soldiers in T-1 tanks could be endangered by alloys in the frame which tend to melt in the heat of the shell-fire.

4. The "memo" below violates many manuscript conventions. Find all errors, including spelling and punctuation mistakes; be very rigorous.

```
To Unit Chief, Re:  Machines

In response to your directive I have looked into the problem of the
water leaks in machine #4 of the Harrison Building, which took place
last Wednesday.  Most of the machines in Harrison have had leakage proble-
ms.  XXXXXXXXXXXXXXXXXXXXXXXX    Last year alone, #1 was out for an        First,
entire month, and we lost #6 completely. /I have reviewed the mainten-       /
ance question.  It appears, however, that the same team maintains these
machines as works on the machines in the Smith building, and there we
have a much better record, even though these machines  (the ones in the
Smith Building)are oler.  Another possibility was that a
certain manufacturer's model might be more XXXXXXXXXXXXXXXXXXXXXXXXX
fragile than others', but this too proved to be a faulty assumption:
#1, #6, and #4, curiously enough, were all made by different companies.  Other
machines made by each of these companies are located around the plant,
and there have been no complaints about them.
        It become apparent then that something in the Harrison Bldg.
itself was causing the problem.  I checked it out for vibration, and
it turned  out that the machines were being subjectedto tremors far be-
```

Section 2.   Spelling

The difficulties, and apparent inconsistencies, of English spelling are well known. Professionals are expected, nonetheless, to spell correctly. There are a few guides which may be followed.

Latin Loan Words

English is consistent in its spelling of words it has borrowed from Latin, via French. (The words have also remained relatively true to their ancient meanings, so that a knowledge of basic Latin vocabulary is helpful in learning English. A reference work on Latin and Greek loan words is included in the "Further Reading" list at the end of Appendix II.)

The Latin word *spectare* ("to look") may be used as an example. Derived English words include *aspect, expect, inspect, suspect, respect, prospect, perspective, retrospective, spectacle(s), spectator*, etc. Only in *expect* does the spelling change (because the consonant cluster *-xs* is not

TABLE A1. *Common Latin prefixes*

Prefix	Meaning	Example	Spelling variations
ab-	from, away	abject	abstract*
ad-	to, toward	advent	aspect†, accident, affirm, aggregate, allocate, announce, approach, attract
con-	with, together	concede	collect, commit, compare, correct
contra-	against	contravene	
de-	down, away	deflect	
dis-	not, apart	distract	divest†, differ
ex-	out, out of	express	evoke†, eccentric, effluent
in-	in/inside, not	induce	imbibe, illogical, immense, impede
inter-	between, among	interrogate	
ob-	toward, against	object	omit†, occlude, oppose
per-	through, by	perfect	
pre-	before	predict	
pro-	for, forward	promote	
re-	back, again	repel	
retro-	backward	retrogress	
sub-	under, down	submit	suspect†, suffer, suggest, suppose, surround
trans-	across, over	transpose	transcribe†

* *s* added before *t* or *c*.
† Final consonant in prefix dropped before certain initial consonants.

used in English). Similarly, from the Latin stem *scribere* ("to write"), English takes *transcribe, prescribe, inscribe, describe,* etc.; from the stem, *mittere* ("to send"), *transmit, transmittal, remit, remittance,* etc.

Prefixes such as *re-, pro-,* and *retro-* also remain consistent in spelling. Exceptions are certain prefixes, such as *ad-,* which end in a consonant. This final consonant will sometimes drop away, or change to the consonant which begins a stem—e.g., *ex-* + *mittere* = "emit"; *sub-* + *portare* ("to carry") = "support." A guide to prefixes and their spelling variations is given in Table A1.

Greek Loan Words

Like all European languages, English has borrowed many words from ancient Greek, and the spelling of these words is also consistent. Most borrowings can be found in the sciences, particularly in medicine. We thus obtain "biology" from *bio-* (life) + *-logy* (theory, or study), as well as medical terms such as "dermatology" (study of the skin), "cystoscopy" ("seeing" the bladder), and "appendectomy" (cutting the appendix).

A number of commonly used words come from Greek too. A partial list of familiar stems follows:

anthropo (man)	neo (new)
auto (self)	path/-pathy (suffering)
chrono (time)	phono/-phone (sound)
dia (across)	poly (many)
gram (drawing/writing)	psych (life, soul)
logos (words, speaking)	scope (to see)
-logy (theory)	syn/sym (with, together)
micro (small)	tele (far off)
mono (single, alone)	thesis (proposition, placement)

Long *e*

The best-known guide to spelling in English is a verse learned by all school-children: "*I* before *e*, except after *c*." This refers to the long *e* sound so common in English words, and so variable in spelling. Note that *ei* is often employed after *c*:

belief		receive
grief		deceit
field	but	ceiling
reprieve		receipt
siege		perceive

Words Ending in *y*

Nouns ending in consonant + *y* change to consonant + *ies* in the plural. The same is true of verbs in third-person singular:

Nouns	*Verbs*
democracy, democracies	try, (he) tries
duty, duties	fly, (she) flies
country, countries	pity, (he) pities
company, companies	hurry, (she) hurries

The same is *not* true when the noun or verb ends in vowel + *y*: *guy, guys* (noun); *obey, obeys* (verb).

-*Es* Endings

English speakers cannot pronounce *s* following these sounds: *ch*, *sh*, *s(s)*, or *x*. The plurals of nouns, and the third person singular of verbs, ending in these sounds are made with *es*:

Nouns	*Verbs*
torch, torches	touch, (she) touches
bush, bushes	push, (he) pushes
mass, masses	pass, (she) passes
tax, taxes	relax, (he) relaxes

Silent *e*

English's silent *e* is usually preceded by a single consonant, and the consonant is usually preceded by a single vowel (though rarely *e*). Examples include *ride, life, define, home, wrote, ate, rule, precede,* and *tyke.* The function of the silent *e* is to make the preceding vowel sound long. Thus, English speakers immediately see different pronunciations for *bit* and *bite, fat* and *fate, rot* and *rote, cut* and *cute.* Usually there is no *e* after a double consonant, partly because the double consonant makes the preceding vowel short: *burr, call, mess, moss, hill* (see below, "Doubling consonants").

The silent *e* is usually dropped before -*ed,* -*ing,* or other suffixes beginning with a vowel:

hide, hiding; smile, smiling
like, liked; ache, ached
rude, ruder; vote, voter
debate, debatable; note, notable
precede, precedent; prude, prudent
incise, incision; locate, location

Sometimes the silent *e* will remain to keep a *c* or *g* preceding it soft: *changeable, embraceable.*

Plural of Words Ending in *f*

Historically, English has had a tendency to form the plural of one-syllable words ending in *f* with -*ves.* This is no longer true of *roof* (*roofs*) and some other examples. Several important words—*wife, life, shelf*—still follow the rule, however.

The -*self* suffix of reflexive pronouns also still takes -*ves.* Thus we have *myself, yourself, himself, herself,* and *itself,* but *ourselves, yourselves,* and *themselves.* Finally, the *f*/*ves* relationship applies to certain words used as both nouns and verbs: *grief*/(he) *grieves, life*/(she) *lives, relief*/(he) *relieves, strife*/(she) *strives, proof*/(he) *proves.*

Doubling Consonants

A final consonant may be doubled before a suffix beginning with a vowel, to keep a preceding vowel short. If the past tense of *admit* were *admited* rather than *admitted*, for example, English speakers would likely pronounce a long *i*. Examples of doubled consonants:

hop: hopped, hopping, hopper (cf. *hope, hoping*)
rid: ridded, ridding, riddance
transmit: transmitted, transmitting, transmitter, transmittal

The rule applies only to accented syllables, however. Note the single consonant in *préference, déstined,* and *óffered,* as opposed to *transmítted.*

Exercises

1. From the guide to Latin prefixes in Table A1 above, experiment with the formation of Latin words. Combine the prefixes in the first column with stems (*-ject, -vent, -press,* etc.) found in the third column. Look up each word, its spelling, and its meaning, in the dictionary; if there is a spelling variation, can it be explained?

2. The eighteen Greek loan words or word-parts listed above can be combined into many English words. Form as many such as you can. Because there are occasional variations in spelling, check the words in the dictionary. *Mono* and *logos,* for example, are combined as "monologue"; the ending *-scope* changes to *-scopy* when a procedure (e.g., "cystoscopy") is meant; and so on.

3. Below is a partial list of words which are often misspelled. It is suggested that each be written in a sentence, or practiced until learned.

accidentally	government	relieve
accommodate	grievous	repetition
achievement	height	resistance
acquire	incredible	schedule
address	intelligence	separate
a lot	judgment	similar
all right	knowledge	succession
apparent	legitimate	technique
argument	manual	temperature
believe	maintenance	tendency
category	mathematics	twelfth
comparable	mischievous	unusually
conscious	necessary	usage
cylinder	noticeable	vacuum

description	occurrence	valuable
exaggerate	precedence	wholly
exceed	privilege	women
February	quantity	writing
foreign	receive	yield

Section 3. Punctuation

Punctuation marks are signals to the reader. With the occasional exception of the comma, they all give a particular message: The period shows the end of a sentence or of an abbreviation; the question mark always indicates a question; and so on. After examining the comma, this section defines precise purposes for several other marks.

Commas

Because there is much variation in the use of commas, English stylists argue over their number and placement. Modern writers use fewer commas than did nineteenth-century writers. Some, for example, do not see a need for the last comma in a series of words or phrases:

> New York is crowded, bustling, and noisy.
> The golfer's shot fell from the sky, landed on the green, and rolled toward the hole.

Such writers will use commas only where they are necessary to give the meaning of a sentence correctly.

The first purpose of commas must be to make meaning clear. A more general rule is to place commas between natural divisions of the sentence, as follows:

1. *Introductory phrase or clause.* Place a comma after a phrase or clause which precedes the main idea of the sentence:

> About 8 p.m., the wind came up.
> Disappointed by his raise, Hawkins complained to his superior.
> Although she had forgotten the man's name, Lisa greeted him like an old friend.

2. *Long clauses.* When a sentence has long, nonrestrictive clauses (see 5 below), divide them with a comma:

> The manuscript had been submitted to the editor the previous week, but Jones still wanted to make a few revisions.

3. *Parenthetical elements.*   Any word, phrase, or clause which interrupts the natural flow of a sentence should be surrounded by commas (or parentheses or dashes; see below):

> I thought, frankly, that you had made a mistake.
> Deegan called Wilson, his clerk, into the office.
> We could see, from the top of the bridge, almost the entire bay.

4. *Parallel items.*   A series of items—numbers, words, phrases, and even clauses—must be divided, usually by commas:

> They cost $15, $12, and $7, respectively.
> She spends her time reading, walking her dog, and working in her garden.
> The embezzler said that he was sorry, that he would never steal again, and that he would repay the firm.

5. *Nonrestrictive clauses.*   Relative clauses (see Appendix III), when they are used to add information about a person, place, or thing mentioned in the main clause, must be set off by commas:

> Peter, who had eaten too much, got sick.
> We sat by the river, which flowed smoothly by.

Note that relative clauses which identify a person, place, or thing must *not* take commas:

> The man who had eaten too much got sick.

6. *Quotations.*   Exact words of a speaker are divided, by a comma, from words about the speaker in the same sentence:

> Jones said, "I don't have time."
> "Please," she said, "come into my office."

Unlike the practice in other languages, English also uses the comma to show a number in thousands—1,152; 2,640,000—but the period to show decimals: 6.2 m.; 7.25%.

See also "Semicolons," below.

Hyphens

The hyphen (-) functions to break a word at the end of a line or to join two words. Sometimes the words joined are single numbers (*twenty-two*), and sometimes one of the words is a prefix which cannot stand by itself; examples include *ex*-husband, *self*-study, and *post*-operative. Two more common uses are described below.

Word breaking.   A hyphen is used to break a word at the end of a line, so that the right-hand margin may remain consistent. A word can be correctly broken only between syllables, which may be determined by speaking the word aloud:

insubordination: in-sub-ord-in-a-tion

ambivalence: am-bi-val-ence

categories: cat-e-gor-ies

Occasionally there is room for judgment. *Insubordination* might be broken between *r* and *d* (*insubor-dination*). It could not, however, be broken into *ins-ubordination*, because the *s* belongs to the *ub* both historically (*sub* is a Latin prefix) and phonetically.

Some long words cannot be broken, because they have only one syllable. Such a word is *straight*; if there is no room for it at the end of a line, *straight* should be written whole on the next line.

Generally, one should not break a word so that only one or two letters appear on either the first line or the second line:

INCORRECT

in-subordination   e-viction

poli-cy   compan-y

It is also considered inappropriate to end three (or more) consecutive lines with word-breaks. Two should be the maximum.

Compound words.   English allows us to create new words by joining two or more existing words. Often the two words must be combined with a hyphen, to avoid confusion. Note this curious statement:

INCORRECT   Jenny saw a man eating tiger.

The meaning is not clear. Since people do not usually eat tigers, it must be assumed that the writer means, "Jenny saw a man-eating tiger." The noun *man* is actually part of an adjective describing the tiger.

The usual function of compound words is to form such adjectives, and often the adjective begins with a noun: *sex*-oriented films, *street*-smart kids, *horse*-show ribbons. At other times it will begin with a verb (*go-getter*) or another word. Compounds such as *bride-to-be, happy-go-lucky,* and *a not-so-funny comedy* indicate the variety of possibilities.

Word combinations should be hyphenated whenever there is a chance that, unhyphenated, they will delay the reader's understanding.

Dashes

Whereas hyphens connect words, or parts of words, dashes (—) divide groups of words or ideas. They show an interruption in the main idea of the sentence; usually it is an interruption which the writer wants to emphasize. The following may be considered models:

> Jensen—not Elliston—broke the gear.
>
> The weather was hot—indeed, torrid—in Arkansas that week.
>
> Please state—carefully, and briefly—your views.
>
> All personnel—administrators, teachers, classified staff, and students—are to be excused at 3 p.m.

Please compare dashes with colons, which are discussed below.

Dashes are not meant to substitute for other punctuation marks. Use them sparingly. A large number of dashes suggests that the writer is engaged in constant self-interruption, and therefore has not organized his or her thoughts.

Parentheses

Whereas dashes emphasize, parentheses de-emphasize. Grammatically, they have approximately the same function—to enclose an interruption—but the idea in parentheses is not essential in the sentence.

Parentheses are useful to report writers. They may enclose the explanation of a term, a reference, a detail which makes a fact specific, etc.

> The broken generator (#9) will be repaired shortly.
>
> The center for *haute couture* (high fashion) is probably New York, not Paris.
>
> Passive solar collectors (see p. 19 of the catalogue) are probably the best solution.
>
> Delivery was promised before June 30 (by their salesman, Joe Ward).

Sometimes an entire sentence, with end punctuation, can be enclosed within parentheses:

> Delivery was promised before June 30. (Shapiro Brothers has a poor history of making deliveries on time, however.)

Commas and other internal punctuation may not precede the closing parenthesis. The closing parenthesis mark may never begin a line, and the opening parenthesis mark must never end one.

Colons

Colons (:) are a sentence-combining device, for they always signal the elaboration of an idea just presented. By "elaboration," two functions—listing and restatement—are meant.

Lists. The colon often signals a simple list of items discussed in general terms before the colon. The "list" may contain just one item:

> There's only one thing Shaw likes: money.

At other times, the list may be a series of grammatical constructions:

> Ms. Collins has four tasks: to meet the client, to show him the plans,
> to persuade him to accept them, and to bring me the contract.

As with all series, the list must contain parallel structures. The above example could be changed to read:

> Ms. Collins has four tasks: meeting the client, showing him the plans,
> persuading him to accept them, and bringing me the contract.

However, it would be incorrect to mix infinitives (e.g., "to meet") with gerunds (e.g., "showing").

Restatement. The colon is sometimes followed by a sentence which restates the words preceding it:

> The company had a good reason not to build a new plant: It couldn't
> raise the capital.

(The first word of the sentence after the colon is capitalized here, but other writers may choose to begin with a small letter.)

Occasionally a dash is used for a function similar to the colon's, as in the following pair of sentences:

> McCullough made a mistake: He got drunk.
> McCullough made a mistake—that is, he got drunk.

Generally, however, their uses are separate. The colon should *not* be used for a list or restatement which simply interrupts the sentence:

> INCORRECT The police found several weapons in the apartment:
> rifles, handguns, and knives, as well as Nazi flags.

The colon cannot be used here unless the sentence ends with *knives*. Otherwise the sentence must be written with dashes:

> The police found several weapons in the apartment—rifles, handguns,
> and knives—as well as Nazi flags.

Finally, the colon cannot be used to start a new line: It must stay with the words which precede it. Like the period, it is then followed by two type-spaces.

Semicolons

Because the colon may signal a restatement, and the semicolon (;) joins two closely related ideas, their functions occasionally overlap. Usually, however, they serve different purposes, and should not be confused.

Even more than the colon, the semicolon is a sentence combiner, in both of the cases discussed below.

Joining main clauses.   Sometimes two ideas of almost equal importance are so closely related that they should not be separated into two sentences. They can be joined by a conjunction (e.g., *and, but, for, or*); sometimes, however, it is better to join them with a semicolon.

The following examples show the semicolon used correctly to join two independent clauses:

> The engineer didn't jump; he stayed with the engine.
>
> Record-players often break down; usually, their owners haven't kept them clean.
>
> Radios provide a lot of entertainment at little cost; they are also relatively durable.

Because semicolons are often used wrongly, incorrect examples are also provided:

> INCORRECT   When you have an accident; wait for the police.
>
> INCORRECT   The medical team observed the child; struggling for air.
>
> INCORRECT   Dawkins, who was our unit chief; they picked him.

In each case, one side of the semicolon or the other does *not* contain an independent clause. Thus, the use of a semicolon is incorrect.

Series.   In the first two incorrect examples above, semicolons have replaced commas, which were the proper punctuation mark. This is a frequent mistake, and nonnative speakers (or native speakers) who do not understand the difference between the two symbols should avoid the semicolon.

There is only one situation in which the semicolon is a proper substitute for the comma, and this situation is a series in which there are already commas. Note the difficulty of this passage:

> The group included Adams, the chief accountant, Crosby, the sales manager, Young, a design specialist, Voorhees, the engineering supervisor, and Dombroski, the director of public relations.

Is Voorhees the engineering supervisor or a design specialist? So many commas confuse us. The sentence contains a series of five items, in each of which there is already a comma. To separate the items, we should use semicolons:

> The group included Adams, the chief accountant; Crosby, the sales manager; Young, a design specialist; Voorhees, the engineering supervisor; and Dombroski, the director of public relations.

The semicolon must stay with the word which precedes it; it cannot start a new line. It is followed by a single type-space.

Apostrophes

The apostrophe (') has two main functions: to show the omission of a letter or letters in a word, and to show possession. It is also used as a substitute for quotation marks, as discussed below (see "Quotation Marks").

Contractions.   Spoken English is full of contractions (words shortened by the omission of letters), particularly in common verbs. "They would" is often pronounced "they'd," as is "they had." "He's" may mean "he is" or "he has," and we even hear "he'd've" for "he would have," or "he won't've" for "he will not have."

Most of these contractions should be avoided in formal writing. The following are acceptable, although not desirable:

> I'm, you're, he's (for *he is*), she's, it's, we're, they're; isn't, aren't; wasn't, weren't; don't, doesn't, didn't; won't, wouldn't; can't, couldn't; shouldn't; mustn't, hasn't, haven't, hadn't

Note that there is no space before or after an apostrophe.

Possessive.   The rules for possessive case formed with apostrophes are generally simple. Singular takes *'s* even when the word ends in *s*, *ss*, *ch*, *sh*, or *x*: *James's*, *boss's*, *torch's*, *bush's*, *tax's*. Plural takes only the apostrophe: *boys'*, *ladies'*, *taxes'*.

There are two major exceptions:

> Possessive adjectives take no apostrophe: *my*, *your*, *his*, *her*, *its*, *our*, *their*, *whose*.
>
> Certain plurals do not end in *s*, and therefore take *'s* in the possessive: *men's*, *women's*, *children's*; *mice's*, *sheep's*, *cattle's*; *alumni's*, *phenomena's*, *data's*.

Remember that *whose* is different from *who's*, as is *its* from *it's*.

Apostrophes cannot appear at the beginning of a line, nor at the end except in a possessive plural like *boys'*.

Quotation Marks

We insert quotation marks to show not only direct quotations of other's words, but also titles and, occasionally, a word which seems unusual in context. Quotation marks must be used whenever the writer borrows another person's words.

Arrange quotation marks with other punctuation according to the following rules.

1. Always place *commas* and *periods* inside quotation marks.

> "Wait," the policeman said. "Open your briefcase."
> The song was called "Love Me Tender."
> Jeff couldn't play "Serenade," but he offered to play "Hard Times."

2. When a quotation is a question, place the *question mark* inside quotation marks; if the quotation is only part of a question, the question mark is placed outside.

> Steve asked, "Are you going to the convention?"
> Have you seen "Wild Strawberries"?
> Is "Who's Afraid of Virginia Woolf?" an interesting play?

The rules for question marks also apply to *dashes* and *parentheses*.

> "What have you—" Jensen didn't finish the question.
> "Will you tell me"—she paused—"why you are so rude?"
> "I won't do it," Harvey said. (To himself he added, "I hope.")
> The manual says, "Press the release button (see diagram)."

3. *Colons* and *semicolons* always appear outside quotation marks.

> Miller had a "shopping list": He wanted 50 revisions, better graphics, and so on.
> In Milan, we saw "Aida"; in Vienna, "Der Rosenkavalier."

4. Occasionally we must put *quotes within quotes*. A title, for example, may be included in a quoted passage. The convention in American (not in British) English is to use the apostrophe or single quotation mark for these internal quotes:

> Ferris asked, "Who has seen 'Annie'?"
> The President said, "Shakespeare's 'sceptered isle' has been our faithful ally."
> "Is 'Help' one of the best Beatles songs?" she asked.

The same conventions apply to internal quotation marks as to external quotation marks. A line cannot end with the begin-quotation mark, nor begin with the end-quotation mark.

Exercises

1. The following sentences each contain a least one mistake in punctuation. It is suggested that, in correcting them, you rewrite the sentences entirely.

- **a.** There are three partners; Manny, Moe, and Jack.
- **b.** "Coming Home, was an award winning film."
- **c.** Make a note of it's arrival.
- **d.** The default was'nt just a mistake:It was a crime.
- **e.** Inspect the circuit breakers (box #9,) and report back to me.
- **f.** Holmes asked "Have you read the marketing reports yet"?
- **g.** We saw the foremen: Hurt and Schwartz, and asked them to explain.
- **h.** The letter was filed under "Accounts Receivable".
- **i.** Jone's note confused me.
- **j.** The letter stated, 'The term "malicious" is too strong.'
- **k.** Pain killing medicines can be addictive.
- **l.** The mechanic stood in the truck bay; just loafing.

2. The following passage has no punctuation. Extra space has been left between words so that punctuation can be added wherever needed.

The term anthropology may be applied to three different professions archaeology which is actually the study of artifacts that is things constructed by humans through the centuries human biology which is principally interested in humankinds evolution as organism and cultural or social anthropology which studies peoples behavior in society the last of these fields although it may look occasionally into historical backgrounds is most concerned with people today it researches their habits their thoughts and their behavior in an attempt to find meaningful patterns

A cultural anthropologist might state the scientific basis of his or her profession this way around the world humankind has developed traditions myths and customs which bear great similarities to one another or at least reflect strong subconscious needs even so called primitive societies have customs which can be compared to those of advanced communities therefore the more we anthropologists study other societies ways the more we learn about our own

But how does social anthropology differ from sociology first anthropologists work on a smaller scale being less interested in statistically based facts than in

activities which cant be quantified secondly anthropologists observe their facts that is their people they may
even participate in the peoples activities finally they
are as interested in what the people believe as in
what they do

Nevertheless social anthropology draws on sociologists
work as it draws on the research of other professions
it works perhaps most closely with linguistics for a
good reason culture and language are interrelated political science economics and psychology are other professions which have well developed ties with anthropology
and last but not least we must mention the two dis-
ciplines with which social anthropology is most often
confused human biology and archaeology

Further Reading

American Chemical Society. *Handbook for Authors*. Washington: American Chemical Society Publications, 1967

American Mathematical Society. *A Manual for Authors of Mathematical Papers*. Providence, R.I.: American Mathematical Society, 1973

American Medical Association. *Stylebook-Editorial Manual*. Chicago: American Medical Association, 1976

Burriss, Eli E., and Lionel Casson. *Latin and Greek in Current Use*. Englewood Cliffs, N.J.: Prentice-Hall, 1963

Council of Biology Editors Style Manual Committee. *CBE Style Manual*, 4th ed. Arlington, Va.: Council of Biology Editors, 1978

Government Printing Office. *Style Manual*. Washington: Government Printing Office, 1982

Hodges, John C., and Mary E. Whitten. *Harbrace College Handbook*. New York: Harcourt Brace Jovanovitch, 1972

Martin, Anne V., Beverley McChesney, Elizabeth Whalley, and Edward Devlin. *Guide to Language and Study Skills for College Students of English as a Second Language*. Englewood Cliffs, N.J.: Prentice-Hall, 1977

University of Chicago Press. *Manual of Style*. Chicago: University of Chicago Press, 1969

Appendix III

Grammar Handbook

The term "grammar" must be treated carefully. Most simply, it refers to the rules of a language, and so a complete grammar is a very large book. Here we can only address certain major problems encountered by speakers of English as a second language.

A grammar, and "grammar rules," also require a large terminology— words like "clause," "modifier," "gerund," and so on. People do not have to know the word *gerund* in order to use gerunds correctly. Obviously, many English speakers have never heard the word, although they repeatedly use gerunds in everyday speech. A student of the language must deal with such terms to understand English sentences, however, and for this reason they appear in the pages which follow.

This grammar handbook is divided into two sections: (1) Sentence Parts, and (2) Sentence Faults; each has its own set of exercises. The terms under each are introduced in alphabetical order.

Section 1.   Sentence Parts

A large percentage of the English grammar is included in the category of sentence parts. Much of it must be omitted entirely here, but a few grammar points which cause nonnative speakers trouble are treated at length. Thus, articles and verb forms receive considerable attention below. Attention is also given to clauses, conjunctions, modifiers nouns and pronouns, objects, prepositions and prepositional phrases, and subjects.

Articles

The English articles *a/an* and *the* have proved to be very difficult for some nonnative speakers, but must be used correctly.

The indefinite article. The article *a* (*an* before a vowel—an apple, an ear, an Indian, an orange, an umbrella) means *one*, unemphasized. Therefore, it can be used only with "count nouns": We can't say "one water" or "one furniture," and thus we can't say "a water" or "a furniture." *A* is also indefinite:

> He turned on a light.
>
> Do you have a book on real estate taxes?

No specific light or book is identified.

Because it means "one," *a* has no plural. Sometimes no article or adjective is used with indefinite plural nouns:

> Do you have books on real estate taxes?

At other times, the words *some* or *any* are used, as follows:

> I have some books. (affirmative)
>
> I don't have any books. (negative)
>
> Do you have any books? (interrogative)

In short, *a/an* cannot be used with a plural noun, nor with a non-count noun such as *water, equipment,* or *information,* nor with a noun which is somehow defined already (e.g., through previous mention). It is normally used with singular count nouns which are not definite, identified, or limited in number: an experiment, a beaker, a mechanical engineer, a city, a forest, a tree, a research paper, and so on.

The definite article. Once the indefinite noun has been introduced, it is afterward referred to as *the* (experiment, beaker, etc.):

> *A man* has been arrested for disorderly conduct. *The man*, identified as Jack Daniels, pleaded "Not Guilty."

This is true also with plural nouns, and usually, with non-count nouns:

> Our laboratory has been conducting *experiments* on recombinant DNA. The results of *the experiments . . .*
>
> *News* has reached us from the battlefield, and *the news* is not good.

Persons and unique things or ideas, on the other hand, are defined by their names. Accordingly, they will take either no article (usually, names of people, cities, continents, countries, lakes, parks, streets) or *the* (buildings, geographical regions, oceans, rivers, seas): the Atlantic Ocean, the Empire State Building, the Mississippi River.

Be alert also to the use of *the* with a generic noun: "the Korean" meaning Koreans as a group, "the automobile" referring to all automobiles, and so on. In addition, *the* is used in comparisons:

> Between those two boys, Jim is the better writer.
>
> Jill is the best poet in the state.

The reason is, again, uniqueness. There can be only one "best poet," and between two writers, only one can be "the better."

Often, persons or things are identified at the time they are introduced, and *the* again becomes appropriate. The italicized words in the following examples show identifying terms:

> The *only* newspaper I have is two days old.
>
> The man *with Mrs. Maze* is our landlord.
>
> The casing *of engine #2* is cracked.

In cases such as that in the second sentence, *the* works like *this* or *that*, as a demonstrative pronoun (see below, "Pronouns").

In some instances, the need for *the* is not clear. Native English speakers say "the post office" even in a city where there are many post offices. Somewhat indefinite nouns will also take *the*: "The point is to leave now"; or "With the assistance of the police, I recovered my car." But for the most part, *the* indicates an understanding between writer and reader (or speaker and listener) that the person, place, thing, or idea is already known, or will be identified immediately.

Clauses

The clause is the smallest unit of the sentence containing both a subject and a verb (see below). Sometimes the clause is "independent"—it can stand alone as a complete sentence:

> s   v
> He walks every day.

Sometimes it is dependent and must be attached to the main (independent) clause:

>   s   v
> He walks every day, while his wife sleeps.

Dependent clauses are divided into three categories: adjectival clauses, usually known as relative clauses; adverbial clauses; and more rarely, noun clauses (see below, "Nouns and Pronouns").

Relative clauses. Relative clauses begin with *who* or *which* or a variation (*whom, of whom, whose, of which, that,* etc.) and describe some person, place, thing, or idea:

> Mr. Perkins, to whom the letter was addressed, has left the company.
>
> Please work this morning for Ms. Winocur, whose secretary is ill.

Note that, in the first example, the relative clause separates the subject and verb of the main clause. In both cases, the relative clause is separated from the main clause by commas (see section on punctuation in Appendix II).

Sometimes, however, the relative clause is needed to identify what it describes; in such cases, no commas are used:

> The man to whom the letter was addressed has left the company.
> The book which you gave me has been very helpful.

In cases like the second example, *that* may replace *which*:

> The book that you gave me has been very helpful.

Relative clauses may also be "reduced," first by removing *that*:

> The book you gave me has been very helpful.

In other cases, relative clauses may be reduced to phrases:

> The shelves which contain non-fiction books are to the left.
> The shelves *containing non-fiction books* are to the left.
> An engine which has an oil leak will cause problems.
> An engine *with an oil leak* will cause problems.

(See also "Prepositional phrases" and "Verbs.")

Adverbial clauses.   Clauses which explain the action in the main clause are called "adverbial." They may show cause, degree, effect/purpose, time, contrast, or condition:

> We couldn't go *because our car broke down.*
> He is free to leave, *except that he must give me his notes.*
> Frank hired more guards, *so that the jewels would be safe.*
> Nero fiddled *while Rome burned.*
> The president will be angry *if he hears of this accident.*

All of the examples contain one independent and one dependent clause. English sentences may contain two or more of either.

Conjunctions

In English, clauses must be joined by conjunctions. There are a few exceptions (the relative clause being one). Commas do not join clauses, except for series of parallel clauses.

The most common conjunctions which join independent clauses are *and*, *but*, and *or*:

> He liked the company but he couldn't get a promotion.

Note that they may serve to reduce the second main clause:

> We could go to the ball game or see a movie ("we could" is omitted).
> Architects feel overworked and underpaid ("architects feel" is omitted).

Reduced clauses always have an *implied* subject or an implied verb or both.

Ambiguous conjunctions. Many conjunctions introduce adverbial dependent clauses. Among the best known are six which have two meanings or functions. The first is *so*, which is most often used as an intensifying adverb (e.g., "so big") or as an adverb meaning "that way" (e.g., "I thought so"). As a conjunction showing cause-effect ("The boss said no, so I couldn't go"), it is informal and is usually avoided by good writers.

Four conjunctions indicating a time relationship—*then, as, since,* and *while*—have a second function each. *Then* usually means "next in time" but is also used to show a result:

> They didn't send the book? Then we won't pay them.

Like *so, then* used in this sense is considered informal.

As and *while* both mean "during that time," but *while* may also mean "whereas," and show contrast:

> While the proposal was interesting, it seemed too costly.

As and *since* ("after that time") are often used to show cause:

> They couldn't go, as/since they were waiting for a phone call.

All of these meanings of *as, since,* and *while* are acceptable in formal writing.

The sixth conjunction, *for,* usually appears as a preposition to show purpose: "He was looking for a pencil." Occasionally, it too may be used as a conjunction to show cause:

> We can't attend the meeting, for our compressor just broke down.

The comma after "meeting" is the signal that *for* is used as a conjunction. Other "time" conjunctions which serve as prepositions are *after, before, since,* and *until,* but in these cases their meanings do not change.

Compound conjunctions. Five sets of word-pairs work as conjunctions to join independent clauses, or terms which are reduced clauses. They are *both–and, either–or, neither–nor, as–as,* and *not only–but (also)*:

> Both Robin and Donna are charming.
> They not only cooked dinner but (also) did the dishes.
> He doesn't play as well as she.

Either lamb or pork will taste good.
I like neither wine nor beer.

There are also multiple-word adverbial conjunctions like *inasmuch as, provided that,* and even *in such a way that*:

He performed beautifully, in such a way that the audience became enthusiastic.

A list of such terms follows, divided by function:

Addition	and besides, in addition to which
Cause	for the reason that, inasmuch as, insofar as, in that, to the degree that
Comparison/contrast	as . . . as, rather than
Concession	despite the fact that, granted that
Condition	assuming that, in case, on condition that, provided that, in the event that
Purposes/effects	in order that, in such a way that, so that, such that, with the result that
Examples	for example that
Exception	except that, with the exception that
Restatement	that is (to say), particularly/specifically that
Sequence	before which, during the time that, following which

Among these, "so that" and "such that" are special in being divisible, like *as–as*:

The machine had problems *such that* we couldn't use it.
The machine had *such* problems *that* we couldn't use it.
The machine worked badly, *so that* we couldn't use it.
The machine worked *so* badly *that* we couldn't use it.

The difference between these two conjunctions is that "such that" leads to an adjectival clause, and "so that" leads to an adverbial clause.

Modifiers

Words or groups of words which describe, enumerate, or otherwise qualify other words are called modifiers. Articles "modify" nouns, or occasionally pronouns, as do adjectives. Adverbs modify verbs, adjectives, or other adverbs:

> often ran (adverb modifying verb)
> unusually large (adverb modifying adjective)
> very quickly (adverb modifying adverb)

Adverbs are often formed by adding *-ly* to adjectives: *bad(ly)*, *strong(ly)*, *vicious(ly)*, *appropriate(ly)*, and so on.

Modifiers can be groups of words, such as relative clauses. Participial phrases (see the section on "Participles" under "Verbs") are another example:

> *Struck by a rock*, the president fell.
> *Using a chair*, the police broke down the door.

In the first sentence, the underlined words modify "the president," and so work as an adjective. The words *Using a chair*, in the second sentence, work like an adverb to describe the way in which the door was broken down.

Position.   Generally, modifiers should be placed close to the words they describe. This is particularly true of those serving as adjectives. Thus, relative clauses almost always follow immediately after the person, thing, or idea they modify:

> The boy *who won the spelling contest* has good mathematics ability, too.
> The book *from which we got the answer* is the course text.

Single-word adjectives—*big, pretty, intelligent*—typically precede the words they modify. The main exception comes with the use of special "linking" verbs, like *is/are, become, seem,* and *appear*:

> The old man seems *vigorous.*
> The plant manager became *angry.*

Certain adjectives beginning with *a-* (e.g., *alike, asleep, alive, afraid, alone*) follow linking verbs and do not precede the noun:

> The boy seemed to be *asleep* but he was *awake.*

Other adjectival constructions which come after the modified word tend, like relative clauses, to be placed immediately after them: "the machine *in the far corner*" or "the girl *driving the car.*"

Adverbial modifiers are less restricted, particularly those showing time or frequency. Note these sentences:

> On Sundays, they usually play baseball.
> Usually they play baseball on Sundays.
> They play baseball on Sundays, usually.

An adverbial clause can, in most cases, either precede or follow the main clause.

Series of modifiers. Either type of modifier can be placed in series (see also "Faulty Parallelism" in Section 2 of Appendix III): "the tall, cool, restful trees" or "He ran silently, swiftly, and urgently." Series which follow the modified word generally take *and* between the last two items. Most adverbs are in this category.

Series of modifiers must be parallel; adjectives or adverbs cannot be mixed with clauses or phrases. The following are correct examples:

> We looked in the cupboard, over the refrigerator, and under the table.
> The man was loud, vulgar, and aggressive.

To change "aggressive" in the second sentence to "acting aggressively" would spoil the parallelism.

Comparison. There are comparative and superlative forms of both adjectives and adverbs:

> a prettier flower; the prettiest flower
> a more beautiful flower; the most beautiful flower
> walking more rapidly; walking the most rapidly

In general, short adjectives take *-er/-est* and long adjectives take *more/most*; never use both. Adverbs ending in *-ly* almost always take *more/most*. Note that, in the superlative, the article *the* is usually required.

Nouns and Pronouns

Words for persons, places, things, and ideas are nouns. In sentences, nouns carry most of the information, and each has a special function as subject or object (see sections on "Subjects" and on "Objects," below). Since pronouns substitute for nouns, they have the same functions.

Nouns. Usually, a noun is a single word with either a concrete or an abstract meaning: *ball* or *game, book* or *information, beaker* or *chemistry*. Nouns can also be "collective"—that is, collect several items into one word; examples are *furniture, equipment, company, herd*. Names (Africa, the Alps, Alan) are also nouns.

Sometimes an *-ing* verb form known as a gerund, or a gerund phrase, works as a noun:

> *Smoking* may be dangerous to your health.
> I like *skiing on dry snow.*

Note that a noun like *cigarettes* could be substituted for smoking and a noun like *snow* for the phrase *skiing on dry snow*. (See below for further discussion of gerunds.)

Occasionally, a clause will serve a noun function. Compare these two sentences, where the object of the verb "reported" is italicized in each:

> He reported *a record harvest.*
> He reported *that the harvest broke all records.*

In the second sentence, only the complete second clause answers the question, "What did he report?"

Although rare, a noun clause may actually be the subject of the sentence:

> *Why she's going* is a good question.
> *That he should talk carelessly* makes me angry.

The italicized clause in the second sentence has the same function as a noun like "carelessness," which might replace it.

Pronouns.   A pronoun is a word which substitutes for a noun; therefore, it must agree with the noun in number and sex:

> All *cultures* have a mythology; otherwise, *they* couldn't exist.
> Each *culture* has a mythology; otherwise, *it* couldn't exist.
> Joe can't live with his *wife* or without *her.*

Unlike nouns, however, pronouns take special forms for different cases. Thus, the subject *I* becomes *my* or *mine* in possessive case, and *me* in objective case:

> The book is *mine.*
> Between you and *me*, a strike is likely.

The personal pronouns in possessive case are *mine, ours; yours;* and *his, hers, its, theirs.* Note that unlike other possessive forms (e.g., *Bill's*), they have no apostrophe before a final *s*.

In addition there are reflexive pronouns, which add *self/selves* to a possessive form. They show persons or things acting for or against themselves:

> Bill hurt himself.
> They gave themselves a party.

Occasionally, this form is used for emphasis, as in "She herself couldn't explain her actions."

A frequently used pronoun is the demonstrative pronoun, which shows position—*this* (plural, *these*) for nearness, *that* (plural, *those*) for distance:

> Which books? These?
>
> That's the boy I saw at the game.

The same four words are also used as adjectives: this/that boy, these/those girls.

Other words which work either as pronouns or adjectives are *all, another, any, each, enough, more, most, much, others,* and *some.* Moreover, *any* and *some* can be joined with *-thing, -body,* or *-one* in compound pronouns like *anybody* or *someone* (see "Agreement Problem, Noun-Pronoun" in Section 2).

Objects

Many sentence errors can be avoided if the writer remembers that, with rare exceptions, every noun (or pronoun) must have one of five or six distinct functions in a sentence. An exception is the use of two names for the same person or thing (called "nouns in apposition"):

> We called *Mr. Jones, the banker.*
>
> One can find *arrowroot, an edible starch,* in the West Indies.

Nouns in apposition are reduced relative clauses. In each example above, both nouns have the same function (direct object).

The specified functions of nouns and pronouns are to be subject, predicate nominative (see below, "Subjects"), or various kinds of objects: direct object, indirect object, or object of a preposition. The three kinds of objects are all represented in the sentence below:

> IO   DO   OP
>
> I gave Smith the keys to the car.

Keys are what was given, Smith was the person to whom they were given, and the car is part of a modifier, controlled by the preposition *to,* describing the keys (see below, "Prepositional Phrases").

Definitions for the three types of objects are as follows:

1. The direct object receives the action shown by the verb.
2. The indirect object is the person to whom or for whom the action is done.
3. The object of a preposition works with the preposition to modify a noun or verb.

The indirect object usually precedes the direct object, and is often a pronoun. The object of the preposition should follow the preposition.

Prepositions and Prepositional Phrases

The function words known as prepositions are difficult to translate from one language to another. There are about sixty prepositions (excluding combinations of such words) in the English language: *up, down, in, out, to, from, over, under,* etc. They are not easy to learn, partly because they may have additional functions as adverbs or conjunctions, as described earlier.

Many idiomatic or slang expressions consist of a verb plus an adverb which is actually a preposition:

> find out (= learn or discover)
> make up (= reconcile or compensate)
> tune out (= ignore or stop listening)

The "preposition" is actually a particle, or small word used to give a special meaning to the verb. See "Further Reading" for a reference work on idioms.

"Time" prepositions.   The true preposition connects its object with a noun or verb, in a logical relationship. Thus, the prepositional phrase (preposition + object) works as a modifier. Often it shows a time relationship:

> We'll meet *after lunch.*
> I'll have it done *before 3 p.m.*
> *In 1981,* President Reagan was shot.
> They have lived here *since the 1930s—for 50 years.*

Other prepositions which show time are *during, from, till/until, within,* and *on/upon.* Be alert to different meanings for some of the time prepositions, however: *in* and *on/upon* often indicate a spatial relationship, and *for* may show purpose.

"Space" prepositions.   Most prepositions indicate a spatial relationship. A basic list follows.

above	between	out
across	beyond	outside
against	by	over
along	down	past
among	from	through
around	in	throughout
at	inside	to
before	into	toward(s)
behind	near	under

below	off	underneath
beneath	on	up
beside	opposite	with

Some of these prepositions show a stationary relationship; others show movement. This is the basic difference between *above* and *over*, *at* and *to*, *beside* and *along*, and *inside* and *into*, respectively.

"Special function" prepositions. A third group of prepositions has special functions, although some show time or space as well. *With* is often used to indicate the means of doing something, and *by* indicates the doer:

> The window was broken *by Jones with a hammer.*

For usually shows purpose:

> The man is waiting *for a bus.*

Of relates a part to the whole:

> I broke the lens *of my camera.*

Besides and *with* show addition, whereas *except* and *without* show omission:

> Bill came *with/without Mary.*
> *Besides Bill and Mary,* Tom was there.
> The whole group came, *except Marge.*

Despite indicates concession; more concretely, it expresses an obstacle conquered:

> The game was played *despite the rain.*

Like shows similarity:

> We need hard workers like Joyce.

Do not confuse *like* with *as*, which is normally a conjunction: "Joyce works hard, as a person should."

See also "Participles," below.

Compound prepositions. Multi-word prepositions are common; thus, one hears "in back of" as often as "behind." The list of compound prepositions which follows is divided by function.

| Addition | as well as, in addition to, together with |
| Cause | because of, due to, on account of (informal), owing to (informal) |

Comparison/contrast	compared with, in contrast/comparison to, by contrast/comparison with
Concession	in spite of
Condition	in case of, contingent upon
Purposes/effects	for the purpose of, to the end of
Examples	as in
Exception	aside from, except for, with the exception of
Sequence/Time	prior to, subsequent to, up till/to
Space	away from, in back of, in front of, next to

The prepositional phrase.   The prepositional phrase always has a preposition and an object, and may also contain articles and adjectives, as in "with *the old* hat." As a part of the sentence, the prepositional phrase must meet the rules for other modifiers. Those which modify nouns should follow the nouns immediately:

> The house *with circular windows* is owned by the Robinsons.
>
> He reads books *by the masters of the last century.*

In the second example, the first prepositional phrase modifies the direct object, and the second modifies the object of the preposition in the first phrase.

Prepositional phrases with adverbial functions are less restricted, although their reference and antecedent must be clear:

> *Around the house* the three boys ran, yelling and laughing.
>
> Yelling and laughing, the three boys ran *around the house.*
>
> The three boys ran, yelling and laughing, *around the house.*

Good writers will sometimes start a sentence with an adverbial phrase or clause, as in the first example. This gives variety to their style (see "Choppiness" in Section 2 of this appendix).

In idiomatic English, native speakers often end sentences with prepositions:

> That's all I can think of.
>
> That's the girl I came with.

In written English, such constructions should be avoided. For example, the first sentence could be changed to "I can think of nothing more."

Subjects

The two most important parts of a clause or simple sentence are the subject and the verb. A sentence may be constructed of a one-word subject and a one-word verb:

> Birds sing.

Words added to this simple sentence will serve as modifiers to one of those two words:

> Our favorite migratory birds / sing sweetly in the evening.

The first half of the sentence is called the complete subject, and the second half is called the predicate (or complete verb).

Most sentences and clauses begin with the subject, which is the person, thing, or idea acting:

> *Whistling* makes me confident.
> *What he said* disturbs me.
> *Einstein* wrote about relativity.

In the first example, the subject is a gerund (see below); in the second, it is a noun clause.

A subject may be restated following a linking verb:

> Mitterand became *President*.
> Elizabeth II is the *Queen*.

The restatement is called the predicate nominative.

Other verbs lead to direct objects. Many such verbs, like *hit*, *give*, or *describe*, normally require objects: The car hit the *rail*; Joan gave the book to a *friend*; Douglas described the *sea*. These sentences may be rewritten so that the object becomes the grammatical subject:

> The rail was hit by the car.
> The book was given by Joan to a friend.
> The sea was described by Douglas.

Such sentences are considered weaker than those in which the agent is the grammatical subject, but they are sometimes needed. (See "Passive voice" under "Verbs.")

Verbs

Verbs are the most complex parts of English sentences. They change forms to indicate past, present, future, or indeterminate times—that is, they have tenses. They also change to non-finite forms, thus working as modifiers, subjects, or objects. Certain among them are verbs which can only "help" other verbs.

The topic of verbs is therefore divided into six subtopics: gerunds, infinitives, modals, participles, passive voice, and tenses.

Gerunds.   Verbs are often changed into nouns in technical English. Examine this partial sentence:

The purpose of *studying* this operation . . .

The verb "study" has been turned into a noun through the addition of -*ing*. The phrase "studying this operation" is the object of the preposition *of*.

Such nominalizations are called gerunds and gerund phrases. Note the variety of functions they may serve:

Smoking is dangerous here. (subject)

His worst fault was *gossiping*. (predicate nominative)

Throwing tools is inexcusable. (subject)

In *reviewing the data*, we found several errors. (object of preposition)

The latter two sentences contain examples of gerund phrases.

Gerunds are correctly used in such statements as "The purpose of (*submitting* time sheets, etc.)," "A process for (*refining* coke, etc.)," "The difficulty in (*setting* production schedules, etc.)," and "This is accomplished by (*removing* the slag, etc.)." The four prepositions *in*, *by*, *of*, and *for* often require gerunds as objects.

A verb can be changed to a gerund by the addition of -*ing* (and the removal of silent *e*, where appropriate). The gerund for *is/are* is *being*, as in "There is no excuse for being late."

Infinitives.   The basic form of every verb is the infinitive, which has no tense (time). Thus *to be*, *to have*, *to see*, etc., are non-finite. Such terms occur frequently in professional writing:

Our purpose is *to find* the defect.

To attach the hose, remove the clamp.

The pressure is raised *to produce* crystals.

This gauge allows us *to monitor* the flow.

It is difficult *to substitute* one part for another.

Numerous verbs take infinitives as objects, e.g., "We expected *to find a residue*."

A passive use of the infinitive also occurs frequently, as in the following:

The fruit *is believed to come* from Indonesia. (present time)

The fruit *is believed to have come* from Indonesia. (past time)

The volume *was shown to be* insufficient.

The problem *is thought to originate* in the amplifier.

A special passive construction is the use of "to be _____," to give direction:

> The manual *is to be read* carefully.
> The machines *are to be shut down* at 7 p.m.

These are polite ways of saying "must be read" and "must be shut down." (See below, Passive voice.).

Modals. The helping verbs called "modals" are special because they cannot be used alone. Because their meanings overlap, they are sometimes confusing. They are reviewed in Table A2, which includes examples to show each function. Among them, *could, might, should,* and *would* are used to indicate hypothetical (unreal) cases as well as present or past tense.

With all modals, there is a distinction between forms for past and present times. The present is formed by modal + infinitive without "to" ("must write"); the past is formed by modal + *have* + past participle ("must have written").

See "Participles," below.

Participles. Two important non-finite verb forms are the present and past participles. The present participle has the same form as the gerund (see above): verb + *-ing*, less silent *e*. But its function is different:

> *Smoking* can be dangerous. (gerund)
> *Smoking constantly*, John read the report. (participle)

Smoking is the subject in the first sentence, but merely describes the subject (*John*) in the second. "Smoking constantly" is a participial phrase.

The present participle may also show continuous action ("We are eating"; "They *were walking* along the road"; "He *has been writing* letters"; etc.). It is often used simply as an adjective:

> The *boiling* liquid . . .
> We used a *bleaching* agent.

A participial phrase may follow the noun it describes:

> The mixture *boiling in the cauldron* . . .
> We observed the liquid *seeping through the tissue.*

It should, as here, follow it immediately, however.

The past participle serves a similar function, except that it is passive—that is, it shows the thing or process being acted upon, not acting:

> The *reconstructed* model . . .
> The model *built by the research group* . . .

TABLE A2. *Summary of modals*

Modal	Function	Example	Tense
Can	Permission	The employees can leave now/at 4 p.m.	Present/future; "may" preferred
	Possibility/ capability	Smith can do the work.	Present/future
	Impossibility	These beams can't support the walkway.	Present/future
		They can't have finished so quickly.	Past; "couldn't have" preferred
Could	Permission	The employees could leave if the work was done.	Hypothetical present
		The employees could have left if the work was done.	Hypothetical past
		The supervisor said the employees could leave.	Past
	Possibility/ capability	Smith could do the work if given a chance.	Hypothetical present
		Smith could have done the work if given a chance.	Hypothetical past
		The company believed that Smith could do the work.	Past
		Smith could have done the work.	Past; "might have done" preferred
	Impossibility	These beams couldn't support the walkway.	Past *and* hypothetical present/future
May	Permission	The employees may leave now/at 4 p.m.	Present/future
	Possibility	The machine may break down.	Present/future
		The machine may have broken down.	Past
Might	Permission	The supervisor said the employees might leave.	Past; "could" commonly used
	Possibility	The beams might support the walkway if properly mounted.	Hypothetical present/future
		The beams might have supported the walkway if properly mounted.	Hypothetical past
Must	Necessity	The machinists must finish on time.	Present/future; "had to" must be used for past
	Probability (strong)	The foreman must know something about it.	Present
		The foreman must have known about it.	Past

TABLE A2. (*Continued*)

Modal	Function	Example	Tense
Should	Obligation	Jones should admit her mistakes.	Present/future
		She should have admitted her mistakes.	Past
	Probability (uncertain)	The trucks should be arriving now/at 4 p.m.	Present/future
		The trucks should have arrived at 4 p.m.	Past
	Condition	Should we be late, start without us.	Future
Will	Expectation	The plane will land at 12:03.	Future
	Intention	He will be there at 12:04.	Future; "is going to" a substitute
Would	Expectation	The pilot said the plane would land at 12:03.	Past
		The plane would land on time, except for high winds.	Hypothetical present
		The plane would have landed on time, except for high winds.	Hypothetical past
	Intention	I decided I would go.	Past
		I would go, except for the cost.	Hypothetical present
		I would have gone, except for the cost.	Hypothetical past

We found the salts *crumbled by the extreme heat.*

The elements, *reseparated,* were recombined in differing quantities.

The past participle is irregular in form, so that each must be learned individually. Often the form is that of the past tense (*boiled, constructed*). At other times, past participles are made with the addition of *-en* (*taken, written*). There are also mutations: *find–found, sing–sung, fly–flown.*

The past participle's other use is to form the perfect tenses (see below, "Tenses"): "We have *spoken*," "You had *seen* the answer," "They will have *thought* the problem through."

Certain participles, past and present, serve as prepositions:

They ate pizza *following* the game.

They made no decision *regarding* her application.

Given his talent, Weiss should succeed.

Granted the difficulties, we can do it.

Barring traffic delays, I'll be there on time.

In such cases, the participles do not show action taken by or against the subject, but work with their objects to form adverbial modifiers.

More commonly, participles show action, functioning as reduced relative clauses:

> *Overcome* by emotion, Jenkins sobbed.
>
> *Fighting* back his tears, he looked at Kay.

A special past (or "perfect") form is used when the action of the participle occurs earlier than the action of the verb:

> *Having written* her son, she picked up her book again.
>
> *Having been wounded* in the war, Vic became a pacifist.

When participial phrases serve an adjectival purpose, they must be placed close to the word they modify.

Passive voice.   The typical English sentence contains a subject (the actor, or agent), a verb (a statement of the action), and a direct object (the person or thing acted upon):

> S   V   DO
>
> The company raised its prices.

This is the preferred method of statement, known as "active" voice.

It is possible to restate sentences with direct objects in "passive" voice:

> Prices were raised by the company.

Passive voice is appropriate in two instances: (1) when, as in most science and technical reporting, the person acting is not as important as the thing acted upon; and (2) when the agent is unknown, or should not be identified:

> Independent calculations will be made by each member of the team. (agent not as important as action)
>
> The reagent was introduced at 83° C. (agent unimportant)
>
> Joe Doakes was attacked last night. ("attacker" unknown)
>
> The specimen jars were accidentally washed. (agent should not be identified)

Grammatically, passive voice requires that the object be located in the subject position. The subject, if it appears, is placed after verb + *by*. The verb is constructed by a form of *to be* + past participle:

> Present: The residue *is drained* by pipes.
>
> Past: The annual report *was written* by the president himself.
>
> Future: Measurements *will be taken* immediately.
>
> Present Perfect: Leaks *have been found* at the joints.
>
> Past Perfect: By Wednesday, a line *had been run* between the poles.

Future Perfect: Before Wednesday, a response *will have been drafted*.

In informal communication, *get* may be used to express passive:

The drill gets damaged easily.
Bill got hit by a falling brick.

Because it is informal—and has numerous meanings—*get* should generally be avoided.

Modals (see above) can be converted to passive according to the models below:

Mistakes should be admitted.
The work might have been finished earlier.

Note also that continuous forms, though rare in professional writing, are possible: "The furnaces are being tested"; "The tubes were being stolen by employees."

Tenses. The six English verb tenses usually indicate a period of time when an action occurred. Verbs in past tense (*came, went,* etc.) show a completed action; those in present tense (*come(s), go(es),* etc.) show a current or repeatable action; those in future tense (*will come,* etc.) show an action not yet begun.

The three perfect tenses are more difficult, since they often cover gaps between the other tenses. Present perfect usually indicates a state or action begun in the past but not completed until the present:

I have just finished my report.

In fact, the action or state may not be finished until the future:

I have worked on this report all day (and am still not done).

Or the action may have been completed, but is repeatable:

I have already written three reports (and must write more).

Present perfect is often used in professional writing to show that research on a subject has not yet reached a conclusion:

Hobbs has suggested that enzymes . . .
Much attention has been given to . . .
Scientists have long wanted to find an explanation for . . .

Note, in the second example, the use of passive voice.

Future perfect is rarely used. Generally, it fills a gap between the present and some future time or action:

Before tomorrow noon, we will have completed all repairs.

Before we meet tomorrow, I will have seen the films.

Past perfect, also infrequent, is often interpreted incorrectly by nonnative speakers. The following statement is an example:

INCORRECT   I had been to the bank.

A past time must be established in order to use past perfect, which has a "beyond-past" function. Either of the following sentences is correct:

I got to the bank at 3:30, but it had closed.
The bank had closed before *I arrived*.

The italicized terms show the establishment of a past time; the bank closed at a beyond-past time.

The perfect tenses are all constructed by a form of *have* + past participle. A continuous aspect is constructed, in all tenses, by a form of *to be* + present participle. It shows an incomplete action:

Present: Dinner *is cooking*.
Past: While the master worked, the apprentice *was cleaning*.
Future: We *will be driving* all day.
Present perfect: He *has been clearing* his desk.
Past Perfect: Before you interrupted, I *had been speaking* of my farm.
Future perfect: At two, we *will have been watching* for five hours.

This mode is appropriate only for actions or states which continue across a point of time used as reference.

Exercises

1. Supply the correct article in the blanks.

_____ typewriter is _____ best friend of _____ professional writer. _____ writers of _____ late nineteenth century were quick to discover its benefits. In fact, _____ typewriter's greatest admirer was probably _____ American humorist named Mark Twain. Although he continued to write mainly with _____ pencil—some said it was because he completed _____ greater number of pages that way, writing in _____ large hand—he was among _____ first people to buy _____ typewriter. He felt this was _____ invention which would make _____ profound and lasting change in _____ writing profession. And _____ fact is, it did.

2. Change the italicized words or phrases in the following sentences to clauses.

a. *Filled with coins,* the box probably weighed 50 lbs.
b. *Walking down the street,* Megin saw a robbery.
c. Mr. Costello punished his daughter *for breaking a vase.*
d. We will return the tools *belonging to the McLaughlins.*
e. Schneider hoped *to get a kiss from his secretary.*
f. The suitcase *on the bed* has already been packed.
g. Kennedy, *like Roosevelt,* tried to inspire the people.
h. We read novels *to nourish our imaginations.*
i. Roses are not only beautiful but *fragrant.*
j. *Irritated,* Mrs. Klemen called the police.

3. Reduce the italicized clauses to phrases or other substitutes.
   a. *That he helped us* will not be forgotten.
   b. She caught the burglar *as he was taking her jewels.*
   c. Dan, *who was a reasonable person,* lost his temper.
   d. Evelyn is a woman *who has hundreds of friends.*
   e. I don't like it *that he drinks so much.*
   f. *The repairman telephoned first,* then came to the house.
   g. Joel doesn't have any sense, *and Betty doesn't either.*
   h. *Although his legs are weak,* Al can do the job.
   i. *In case there is a fire,* break the glass.
   j. *Jeannette used a hammer* and quickly broke the lock.

4. In the following sentences, change the verb under each blank to a gerund or an infinitive, and add the correct particle (*by, for, in, of, to/to be*):

   a. The purpose _____ the experiment is _____
                    continue   find
      marketable by-products.

   b. _____ the battery, you will need _____ socket
         remove   have
      wrenches.

   c. _____ on television, we ought _____ our market
         advertise   increase
      share.

   d. The directions are _____ exactly, _____ costly er-
                              follow   avoid
      rors.

   e. A device _____ fuel efficiency seems _____ the best
                   increase   offer
      solution.

   f. _____ the machine, please remember _____ safety
         operate   wear
      glasses.

   g. _____ a portable generator, we improve our
         maintain
      chances _____ a shutdown.
                prevent

5. Expand the following word-groups into sentences with appropriate participial phrases, using past or present participles. A model is given.

> *Example:* rats
> Rats *feeding on sugar-substitutes* have developed cancer.
> Rats *crowded into cages* became aggressive.

   a. We saw the fish
   b. The frame collapsed,
   c. The motor could he heard
   d. Dr. Chung found her experiment
   e. Now observe the ants,
   f. The office,
   g. Atoms
   h. Pesticides, when
   i. When
   j. If

6. Restate the following sentences in passive voice, and judge whether the subject should be kept or dropped.

   a. I have checked all the circuits.
   b. The manager himself had called a meeting.
   c. Dr. Frank will inspect the lab at 4 p.m.
   d. The technician adds the reagent at 3,000 psi.
   e. Jane Doe attacked Joe Doakes.
   f. Somebody has repaired the water pump.
   g. Trudeau mistakenly emptied all the beakers.
   h. Alcohol can remove certain stains.
   i. You are to take these samples away immediately.
   j. An intruder must have broken the lock.

7. Provide a correct form of the verb in the parentheses.

   a. The engineering group (discover) more problems in the new design.
   b. Engine 8 (break) down yesterday; it (run) erratically for a week before that.
   c. (Be) that vehicle ready? We (wait) long enough.
   d. Recent research (concentrate) on lateral loading.
   e. I (be) in London several times.
   f. Soon our attention (draw) to the map.
   g. My investigation (indicate) lasers could (use) successfully; until this point, however, previous efforts (fail).
   h. If this run (finish) in the next ten minutes, we (process) 60 units in only five hours.
   i. The plant (inspect) thoroughly; nothing more needed (do).
   j. What (be) our next step if the experiment (fail)?

Section 2.   Sentence Faults

Twelve common sentence faults are discussed in this unit. They will be more quickly understood if the reader has learned the rules in the preceding unit, on sentence parts.

Agreement Problem, Noun-Pronoun

Pronouns substitute for nouns; therefore, they must "agree" in number and sex with their antecedents (the nouns they replace). The following sentences are obviously wrong:

INCORRECT   Jim was fired by his boss. *They* didn't like his absences.

INCORRECT   Anne drank too much cider. *He* got very sick.

A boss must be, of course, *he* or *she*, and a person named Anne will be a woman.

Indefinite antecedents.   Sometimes the antecedent (the noun which is replaced) is indefinite; the number of persons, or the person's sex, is unknown. It is no longer considered appropriate to use masculine pronouns generically (that is, for all persons or any person):

INCORRECT   If someone has a suggestion, *he* can write us a letter.

The appropriate method is to use a sentence like one of the following:

If someone has a suggestion, he or she can write us a letter.

If people have suggestions, they can write us letters.

Suggestions can be sent by letter.

It may also be acceptable to use "s/he" for "he or she."

The use of the plural *they* (or its variations) as a substitution for special pronouns like *everyone, someone, anyone,* and *no one* is also incorrect in written English:

INCORRECT   Everyone should bring *their* books with *them*.

INCORRECT   Someone is going to find *themselves* in trouble.

INCORRECT   No one can register now; *they* have to wait.

These generic pronouns are always singular. Others like them are *another; everybody, anybody, somebody, nobody; every/any/some/nothing; each; either, neither;* and *none.* Correct examples are:

Anybody has the right to protect himself or herself.

Everything is in its place.

Each has a code number after it.

Vague pronouns. A special problem is the vague pronoun, whose antecedent is not clear. This may be due to the possibility of more than one antecedent:

> INCORRECT   Brown liked skiing, whereas Green preferred horseback riding. Once, he took a bad fall.

We are not sure which man fell.

It is often used vaguely:

> INCORRECT   The deed might have been in a folder which he carried in his briefcase; it was stolen last year.

There are three possible antecedents for *it*: deed, folder, and briefcase.

It, *this*, and *that* are also used too often to substitute, unclearly, for an implied idea or a group of ideas:

> INCORRECT   Joe stayed drunk between Thanksgiving and New Year's and forgot to give his wife a Christmas present. *That* was a mistake.

> INCORRECT   He reports that sales were down in Ontario but up in Montreal. *This* is interesting.

> INCORRECT   I don't mind your wrecking the car or arguing with the police. *It's* not my concern.

Although common in everyday speech, the very broad usage of *it*, *this*, *that*, and other pronouns causes confusion in writing, and should be avoided.

Agreement Problem, Subject-Verb

Verbs must agree in number with their subjects. Except for the verb *to be*, English verbs have no person markers, and therefore, they have only singular and plural forms. The modals (*can*, *should*, etc.), in fact, have only one form, and all verbs except *to be* have only one in past and future tenses:

> Past: He went; they went.
> Past Perfect: She had gone; they had gone.
> Future: He will go; they will go.
> Future Perfect: She will have gone; they will have gone.

The possibility of subject-verb agreement errors exists only in third-person singular and plural of the present and present perfect tenses, but errors do occur.

Collective and abstract nouns. Collective nouns representing groups of people are treated as singular in American English, but not in British

English:

> The government has announced ... (British: The government have
> announced ...)
>
> The team is ready. (British: The team are ready.)

Otherwise, collective nouns—*herd, flock, collection, series*—are treated as
singular in both British and American English. This is true also of abstract
and other non-count nouns. Mistakes occur when such nouns end in -*s*:

> INCORRECT   The news are good.
>
> INCORRECT   Economics have proved a difficult subject.

Compound subjects.   Where there is more than one subject, a plural
verb is needed. Thus, a sentence beginning "Corn and wheat ... " cannot
be treated as singular:

> INCORRECT   Corn and wheat is major American crops.
>
> INCORRECT   My sisters and my mother is coming.

Compound conjunctions like *neither–nor* and *either–or* do not lead to
plural verbs unless the second subject is plural:

> INCORRECT   Either White or Erb have the notes.
>
> Neither his daughters nor his son play the piano.
>
> CORRECT   Neither sharks nor crocodiles make good pets.
>
> Either ignorance or miscalculations are the cause.

Gerund phrases and noun clauses.   A gerund, gerund phrase, or noun
clause takes a singular verb. The following show incorrect usage:

> INCORRECT   Welding take a lot of practice.
>
> INCORRECT   Washing cars don't pay well.
>
> INCORRECT   That he should shout insults are inexcusable.

The exception is, again, a compound subject: two (or more) gerunds
("Welding and riveting"), gerund phrases, or noun clauses.

"There is" and "It is."   Sentences often begin with the expletives "It
is" or "There is," as in "It is my fear that they will lose" (see below,
"Wordiness"). The true subject in either case follows the verb; thus, in
the sample sentence, *fear* is the real subject.

In "It is" sentences, an agreement must exist between subject, verb,
and "it"; plurals are incorrect, or at least awkward:

> INCORRECT   It are our views ...
>
> INCORRECT   It's good deeds that one remembers.

"There is," however, may be changed to "There are," as in "There are
two reasons ... "

Hidden subjects. The major cause of subject-verb agreement problems comes from an assumption that the subject is the noun preceding the verb. Often, this noun (or pronoun) is not the subject:

> INCORRECT   A band of thieves are roaming the streets.

"Thieves" is an object of a preposition; "band," which is singular, is the subject. (See "Subjects" in Section 1.)

Dependent clauses which separate the subject and verb of the main clause may cause errors like the following:

> INCORRECT   Someone *who can arrange the flowers and supervise the caterers* are needed.

"Someone," a singular subject, requires the predicate "*is* badly needed."

Be especially careful of collective nouns + *of* + object. The rule is not always strict here. It is appropriate to say, "A number of people are going," even though *number* seems to be singular. Similarly, it is acceptable to say "A group of executives are meeting," even though "A group of executives is meeting" is also correct.

The following, however, are incorrect:

> INCORRECT   A class of sixth graders are coming.
> INCORRECT   A herd of cattle have been lost.
> INCORRECT   A team of basketball players are staying here.

Choppiness

Sentences may be grammatically correct but not satisfying to the reader. A common example is the child's letter to his or her grandparents:

> Dear Grandma and Grandpa,
>   How are you? I'm fine. Dad and Mom are okay. Susie is well too. The weather has been good. We've been playing softball. (etc.)

The word "choppiness" expresses the idea of sentences which are short and mechanical.

There are actually two problems in the child's letter. The sentences are not only very short, but except for the first one, each has a strictly subject-verb structure. Occasionally, writers should start sentences with an adverbial clause, a modifying phrase, or at least a transition ("Therefore," "By contrast," etc.).

Both sentence length and sentence structure need variation. Avoid a long passage in which all the sentences are short, long, or monotonous in structure. Most should begin with subject and verb of the main clause, however, and nonnative speakers should write mainly short sentences until they have fully mastered grammatical structure.

Comma Splice

English tolerates only a few means of joining clauses. The most common is by conjunction; in a sentence of five clauses, there would normally be four conjunctions. A relative pronoun (*who, which*, etc.) will serve as its own conjunction, and a semicolon will replace a conjunction, but a conjunctive element must be present.

Commas do not normally work as conjunctions:

> INCORRECT   Send the report to me, I want to read it.

Although common in the writing of both native and nonnative speakers, this "comma splice" is incorrect. The only major exception is in a series, where commas may be used to set up parallel clauses:

> Jack brought the meat, Fred brought the beer, Ellen brought the salad, and Carol brought the dessert.

Because commas do signal series, the use of a comma splice where a conjunction is needed can cause confusion. (See below, "Faulty Parallelism.")

Sometimes there is not even a comma to join clauses:

> INCORRECT   The ball looked fair however the umpire called it foul.

However is not a conjunction but a transition word. Thus, we have a "run-on" sentence—one which runs on without punctuation.

Dangling Modifiers

Writers, including native speakers, often make embarrassing mistakes in English by placing modifiers in incorrect positions. Several terms are used for various errors: "squinting," "misplaced," and "dangling" modifiers. The last, which means "hanging loosely," will be used here for all cases.

Any modifier—clause, gerund phrase, infinitive phrase, prepositional phrase, participial phrase—may dangle, but the mistake is most often made with a participial phrase. Either the modifier has no noun to "hang from" or it seems to refer to the wrong noun.

Absent reference.   Sometimes writers create actions where there is no agent:

> INCORRECT   Driving down the street, the leaves were so beautiful.

"Leaves" can't drive; the writer assumes the reader knows who is driving.

Other examples are:

> INCORRECT   Paris was lively, *arriving in the spring.*
>
> INCORRECT   Jim didn't appear, *which was disappointing.*
>
> INCORRECT   The set can be repaired *without having to remove the back.*
>
> INCORRECT   *In learning English,* books are only partially helpful.
>
> INCORRECT   *To live healthily,* vegetables and fruits are recommended.
>
> INCORRECT   *As a working man,* Mrs. Lapham complained about his long hours.

In each case, the italicized modifiers lack a term to modify.

Generally, the term which is modified must stand just before or just after the modifier; in the last three erroneous sentences above, the word after the comma should refer to the person who is (1) learning English, (2) trying to live healthily, and (3) employed as a working man.

Incorrect reference.   Dangling modifiers are most confusing when there are two possible references, and the wrong one seems to have been chosen:

> INCORRECT   Mortally ill, the doctor watched the woman writhe on her bed.

Surely it is the woman who is mortally ill. Other examples:

> INCORRECT   The farmer with the big pig, *who wanted to buy my land,* had ten children.
>
> INCORRECT   *While they were sleeping,* bad dreams bothered all the Thompsons.
>
> INCORRECT   Hanson claimed that, *drunk or sober,* ghosts came to his room.
>
> INCORRECT   Ms. Emerson said that her stomach had to be empty *to write well.*
>
> INCORRECT   *Lying at the bottom of the ocean,* the diver found the gold.

In each case, the italicized modifier stands closer to a false reference than to the intended one (e.g., in the last sentence, to *diver*, rather than to the gold on the ocean bottom).

Participial phrases cause the most difficulty because their placement can vary widely. They may modify the subject and yet stand after the direct object, if the reference is clear:

> We bought the flowers, spending our last dollar.
>
> Martha fell on her bed, exhausted.

In both sentences, the commas are necessary. The second example could be improved by placing "exhausted" at the beginning of the sentence. Commas won't always save a dangling participle.

INCORRECT   Ned gazed at his dog, smoking a cigarette.

In summary, it is generally best to place a modifier beside the modified noun.

Faulty Negation

Three types of errors may occur when we turn an affirmative (positive) statement in English into a negative statement: (1) using more than one negative word, (2) failing to add a helping verb, and (3) failing to invert after an emphatic negative word.

Double negatives.   *Not* is not the only English word which shows negation. Others include *never*, *nothing*, *no*, and *none*. Only one of these should be used in a single clause.

Spoken English, particularly among uneducated people, is full of double (or triple) negatives:

INCORRECT   I have*n't* got *no* car.

INCORRECT   We do*n't hardly* ever see him.

INCORRECT   He wo*n't* take *nothing* from *nobody*.

INCORRECT   She *never* saw *none* of them.

Mathematically, two negatives are like (-1×-1); "I haven't got no car" logically means, "I have a car."

In this respect, partial negatives like *hardly* count as full negatives. Other words in this category are *rarely*, *scarcely*, *barely*, *seldom*, and (in some cases) *only*.

Missing auxiliaries.   Particularly in American English, *not* must be preceded with a modal or other helping verb, and followed by the main verb. Thus, we can't say the following:

INCORRECT   They went not to the game.

INCORRECT   The tulips not blooming.

INCORRECT   Not ask any more questions.

An occasional exception is found with the verb *have*, where it is possible (but not standard in American English) to say, "I haven't any idea."

An existing auxiliary is used in most cases—for example, *have/had* in present and past perfect:

Haven't you seen him?

By 3 p.m., she hadn't come.

In future perfect, where there are two helping verbs, the first (*will*) is placed before *not*: "She will not (won't) have finished by then."

Future tense also uses *will* before *not* ("I won't stand for it"). Regular present and past have no auxiliaries, however, and thus *do* and *did* are needed. "He sings" and "He sang" are made negative as follows:

> He *doesn't* sing (plural: "They don't sing.")
> He *didn't* sing.

Note that in past tense the infinitive form replaces the past form of *sing*. Similarly, "He ran" and "She swam" become "He didn't *run*" and "She didn't *swim*"; etc.

In passive voice, the helping verb for present and past tenses is a form of *to be*. Here are active and passive negatives for "Jones signs the checks":

> Jones *doesn't* sign the checks. (past: *didn't*)
> The checks *aren't* signed by Jones. (past: *weren't*)

As in other cases, passive makes use of the existing auxiliary.

In the continuous form, the existing form of *to be* is used:

The performances *aren't* taking place today.
The committee *hasn't* been working hard enough.

Note that *ain't*, an ancient form of *are not*, is incorrect in formal English.

Be alert to an irregularity in question form:

Aren't you going?
Are you not going?
Haven't the Kellers seen him?
Have the Kellers not seen him?

The contraction *-n't* stays with the auxiliary, before the subject. When fully written (or spoken), *not* must follow the subject.

Lack of inversion.   Negative terms are often used at the beginning of a sentence for emphasis. In such cases, the helping verb precedes the subject. For this reason, the following are incorrect:

> INCORRECT   Never I have seen such a beautiful woman.
> INCORRECT   Rarely one has a chance to talk with a genius.
> INCORRECT   Scarcely I had sat down when the telephone rang.

Instead, follow these models:

Not for a million dollars would I take that job.
Seldom does a company split stock.
Only once has he offered to help.

Strong affirmative adverbs, such as *always* or *frequently*, used for emphasis in the same way (as in "Frequently I walk to the foundry") do not take inversion.

Faulty Parallelism

Good style, which in professional writing is economical style, requires parallel structures in sentences. Parallelism is also needed to avoid confusion. Examples of faulty parallelism are common in everyday writing:

> INCORRECT   The defendant said that he was sorry, that he would not repeat his offense, and the judge reduced the sentence.

To be correct, the sentence requires *and* before the second *that*.

Parallelism refers to a series of words or word groups of the same type; they can be nouns, verbs, adjectives, adverbs, phrases, or clauses. Two such items may be joined by *and*, *or*, or *but* alone. In a longer series, all items are joined by commas except the last, which is preceded by comma + conjunction. (Adverbs and adjectives which precede the subject are exceptions—e.g., "the cold, mournful wind.").

The following are incorrect although not confusing:

INCORRECT   The peasants were hungry, cold, depressed.

INCORRECT   She smiled spontaneously, constantly, sweetly.

Confusion is caused when the items in the series are not grammatically identical. Typical errors are these:

> INCORRECT   The wine is dry, fragrant, and causes no hangovers.
>
> INCORRECT   We'll take Johnson, Boswell, Fielding, but Goldsmith must stay.
>
> INCORRECT   To have a good job, to live in a nice house, and making money are all he wants.
>
> INCORRECT   They changed their clothes, raced downstairs, and the party began.

And in the first example should be followed by another adjective, not a verb. In the second example, the first three nouns are objects of *take*, but *Goldsmith* is the subject of *must stay*. The third example mixes the gerund phrase *making money* in a series begun by infinitives; and the final example introduces a new subject where another verb is wanted.

There are numerous cases where parallelism should be maintained even if its absence is not confusing:

> INCORRECT   We *ran* onto the field, *played* enthusiastically, and *were beaten* by the other team, 16–0.
>
> INCORRECT   Here are good things *to eat* and *for drinking*.

INCORRECT   Give me brooks *which* ripple and fires *that* crackle.

INCORRECT   We like *games, puzzles*, and *being together*.

In the final example, the process "being together" should be changed to "each other's company" or another noun which, like *games* and *puzzles*, is fixed and concrete. The change from active to passive voice in the first example is unnecessary and awkward.

Fragments

An English sentence has a subject and a verb. Without either of these, the sentence is incomplete:

INCORRECT   Sang songs, played games, ate popcorn. (no subject)

INCORRECT   A yellow ribbon on the old oak tree. (no verb)

These examples are only pieces of sentences, or fragments.

Although common in everyday writing and in fiction, fragments are incorrect and should be avoided. Often they reflect an afterthought:

INCORRECT   To build a fire, you need wood, leaves, paper, and kerosene. Also, matches.

Good writers do not have such afterthoughts, since they plan their work before they begin. At least, they rewrite to avoid fragments.

A sentence with a complete clause may nevertheless be a fragment. A common error among nonnative speakers is this sort of construction:

INCORRECT   We were watching a program on the television showed the war in Ethiopia.

The first clause (through "television") is correct, but there is no subject for *showed* in the second clause. It is important to remember that an English noun or pronoun can have only one function: either subject *or* direct object *or* something else. *Television* cannot be both the object of the preposition *on* and the subject of *showed* (see "Objects" and "Subjects" in Section 1). The relative pronoun *which* is needed in the second clause.

Similarly, an extra noun or pronoun causes a fragment. These too are typical errors:

INCORRECT   I am returning the key which you gave me *it*.

INCORRECT   I didn't like the radio, which *it* didn't work.

Which is always a pronoun, even though it makes its own conjunction. In the first example, *which* is the object of the verb *gave*; in the second, it is the subject of the verb *did* (not) *work*. In both cases, the pronoun *it* is not only unnecessary but confusing.

Either a relative pronoun or a subordinating conjunction means that there must be a second clause in a sentence. The presence of either, when there is only one clause, creates a fragment:

INCORRECT   The glass about *which* you spoke.

INCORRECT   *If* he interested, he can go to the play.

INCORRECT   We'll get tickets for the concert *unless* sold out.

The second example reflects a common error. *Interested* is only a participle; *is* must precede it.

Pronoun Shifts

Personal pronouns cause difficulties for writers in the professions. Not only must the pronouns agree with their antecedents, and with their verbs, but they must agree with each other. Note the confusing shift of pronouns in this example:

INCORRECT   We had to give up. You can't teach an old dog new tricks.

The first sentence uses *we* to refer to a given antecedent. *You* in the second sentence, however, means "anyone" or "someone."

The two major complications in the use of personal pronouns are (1) the need for generic pronouns and (2) the perceived need to avoid first-person singular pronouns.

Problems with generic pronouns.   Although the following is awkward, it is better than the example used above.

INCORRECT   We had to give up. One can't teach an old dog new tricks.

One is perhaps the most correct pronoun for the unknown or general agent. In American English, however, *one* is normally not used repeatedly:

INCORRECT   One hates to see one's words used against one.

The second and third uses of *one('s)* would typically be changed to *his* and *him*. Yet this practice is also no longer acceptable, for the unknown person may be a woman (see above, "Indefinite antecedents").

It is difficult, in fact, to find a pronoun which will properly stand for "anyone" or "someone unknown or unimportant" in an extended passage. Both *we* and *you* are so used, but *you* is considered inappropriate in formal writing:

INCORRECT   To begin the experiment, you light the burner . . .

You may in fact be threatening to readers, for it seems to address them too directly.

We is acceptable as a generic pronoun, but a conflict may arise between the generic *we* and a real *we* (with antecedent):

> INCORRECT   Hank and I went to the factory, where we spoke with the manager. We all know that managers never admit mistakes.

The first *we* substitutes for "Hank and I"; the second means "everyone."

A third usage—*they*—is unacceptable. *They* is often used in everyday speech to mean "some authority" or "someone with authority."

> INCORRECT   He couldn't get a job there because they had no openings.

> INCORRECT   They say that a Swedish doctor has found a cancer cure.

In the first case, *they* is vague. In both cases it is informal; the generic use of *they* should be avoided in professional writing.

In summary, *one* is the best choice for a generic pronoun used once, and *we* is the best where several are needed. Whatever the choice, shifts must be avoided.

Avoidance of first-person singular.   When a professional person writes about research he or she has conducted alone, a pronoun problem immediately arises. Many writers dislike using first-person pronouns, as in the following:

> First, I increased the pressure to 6000 psi. I then injected helium. . . .

Because professional, and particularly technical, writing aims at impersonality, writers feel uncomfortable referring repeatedly to themselves.

One alternative is to use passive voice, but this is not recommended for constant use:

> INCORRECT   First, the pressure was increased to 6000 psi. Helium was then injected . . . measurements were taken . . . etc.

Even writers in the sciences and engineering should aim for regular use of active voice.

Sometimes writers choose a second alternative: using *I* only where absolutely necessary and then switching to a generic pronoun. The result may be unsatisfactory.

> INCORRECT   I reported the results to the profession in November, 1981. We can see that the problem . . .

First-person singular is preferable to repeated pronoun shifts or passive sentences.

Repetition

The term "repetition" may refer either to repeated words or to repeated ideas (redundancy).

Repeated words. The unnecessarily frequent use of a word is considered poor style:

> INCORRECT Remove the carburetor from the box and place the carburetor on the engine, using special screws designed for the carburetor.

The first solution to the problem of repetition is the substitution of a pronoun (*it*) for a noun (*carburetor*).

At other times, repetition is avoided by restructuring the sentence. Below are two awkward statements and improved restatements:

> INCORRECT This is a maintenance-free fan. Do not oil the fan.
>
> CORRECT This is a maintenance-free fan, which should not be oiled.
>
> INCORRECT Enclosed is your warranty and an owner's manual. The owner's manual contains . . .
>
> CORRECT Enclosed is your warranty and an owner's manual containing . . .

Good stylists do not begin a new sentence with the word(s) which ended the preceding sentence, as in the second example.

Usually, writers also try to avoid ending consecutive sentences with the same word(s):

> INCORRECT Thoreau liked the *woods*. Life was peaceful in the *woods*.

This repetition could be avoided in several ways, e.g., "Thoreau liked the woods, where life was peaceful."

Synonyms may also prevent the overuse of individual items. Many technical words (e.g., *carburetor*) have no exact synonyms, but substitutions may be made by words representing the general class in which a technical term falls:

> Blenders save a cook's time. These *appliances* . . .
>
> I recommend Ace Spot-Remover. This *product* is . . .

Demonstrative pronouns alone (*these, this*) are less satisfying.

For general terms, synonyms are usually available:

> The building was erected in 1891. The architect of the *structure* was . . .
>
> He faced several hard problems. The most *difficult* was . . .

The writer must be certain, of course, that the original term and the synonym have the same meaning.

Repeating ideas.   Redundancy (saying the same thing twice) is usually an intellectual, not a grammatical or stylistic, fault. Sometimes, however, strong words are incorrectly given intensifying modifiers to make them seem even stronger:

> INCORRECT   very unique ("unique" means "one of a kind"; no intensifier is possible)
>
> INCORRECT   smash heavily ("heavily" is the only way one smashes)
>
> INCORRECT   a large mob of people (mobs cannot be small)

All things considered, intensifying modifiers should be used sparingly.

At other times, redundancy slips into writing without the writer seeing it:

> INCORRECT   Baseball is Angell's *passion*; he really *loves* the game.
>
> INCORRECT   The *stirring* music, written when Tchaikovsky was deeply depressed, *moved* and *excited* the audience.

The same idea has been expressed in two ways, unnecessarily. (See also "Wordiness," below.)

Tense Shifts

Like pronouns, verb tenses must remain consistent in a piece of writing. A confusing shift is seen in these statements:

> INCORRECT   A year ago, Bernice was seriously ill. She is seeking a medical explanation.
>
> INCORRECT   Woyzeck deserted from the Army last year. He will be court-martialed.

The second example, with its jump from past to future, is especially jarring. The first would be acceptable with a transition signal to the reader, such as "*Today*, she is still seeking a medical explanation."

Generally, a report or article adopts either the present or the past as its period, and stays with it. The description of a process or procedure usually maintains present tense:

> The furnace *is cooled* for 8 hours. Workmen then *remove* the slag.

On the other hand, a report on historic events or causes of a problem normally would be written in past tense:

> The engine *began* smoking at 9:15. We immediately *turned* off the power and *stripped* it down.

Writers employing present tense may use present perfect to look back in time, and those writing in past tense will use past perfect for the same purpose. The following sentences, which mix up simple and perfect tenses, are both inappropriate:

> INCORRECT   The foreman was dismissed. He has been neglecting his work.

> INCORRECT   Now place the methyl alcohol, which had been cooling in the retort, . . .

Of course, a piece of writing must often deal with past *and* present, and possibly the future; a report may have a section titled "Background" (past), a section on current situation (present), and conclusions which predict benefits from a proposed innovation (future). In such cases, signal tense shifts with special transitions:

> Having reviewed the causes, we turn to the situation at present.

> This is our present position. What can we expect in the future?

> This is our present position. In the following section, I analyze the factors that brought us here.

Notice that transitions provide for shifts between paragraphs or long sections.

Shifts inside a paragraph—and certainly, inside a sentence—should be avoided. Even a present situation should be described in past tense if the rest of the passage is in past tense. The following is considered awkward:

> INCORRECT   He expressed a wish to see New York and Chicago, because New York is the country's largest city and Chicago has an exciting reputation.

Because of the verb *expressed* (past), the writer should place the two following verbs (*is, seems*) in past tense also.

The rule is seen most clearly in "reported" speech (an indirect quotation). The following sentence seems peculiar but is correct:

> He said he was coming back tomorrow, not today.

The use of "tomorrow" with "was coming" is more correct than the combination of "said" and "is coming" or "will be coming."

Note also that shifts from the regular to the continuous mode of a verb, even in the same tense, are considered awkward:

> INCORRECT   While he *is taking* his walk and *feeds* the pigeons, let's . . .

This is faulty parallelism (see above), as is an unnecessary shift from active to passive voice.

Wordiness

Because professional people like economy in writing, wordiness should be avoided. Technical memoranda may even employ a style which omits articles and some prepositions, and reduces nouns to abbreviations, initials, or even numbers. An example:

> 1400 hrs.: Move CAT scanner to #7.

In any writing of a professional nature, short constructions are preferable to long constructions.

An example of sentence inflation is seen in the rewriting of "I believe" to "It is my opinion that," or even:

> INCORRECT   It is my honest opinion that. . . .

Expletives ("it is," "there is/are") are often sources of wordiness:

> INCORRECT   It is the view of the government that . . .
>
> INCORRECT   There is one candidate who seems sincere . . .

Expletives are often necessary, as in "It is raining," or "There are three Thackeray daughters," but they are overused.

Occasionally, a clause or other long word group can be replaced by a single adjective, conjunction, or other word:

> INCORRECT   These are donuts *which taste very good.* (tasty)
>
> INCORRECT   He smiled *in a manner which didn't convince me.* (unconvincingly)
>
> INCORRECT   *Because of the fact that* she refused his offer . . . (Because)
>
> INCORRECT   *People who love dogs* will object. (Dog-lovers)

Note, in the final example, the possibility of hyphenating two words to form a new word.

Series (see "Parallelism" in Section 1) are meant to reduce the number of words needed to express similar ideas. The following sentences need to be combined:

> INCORRECT   Richard Wagner apparently didn't care about the strain on his singers. He made no concessions to the requirements of stage designers. He felt no need to give his audience a good story.

Several statements are possible, but the most economical is this:

> Richard Wagner made no concessions to his singers, his stage designers, or his audience.

It improves on the original, because the three verbs are basically synonyms, and thus two can be eliminated.

Finally, passive voice is wordy by comparison with active:

INCORRECT   A fastball was thrown to me by Gossage.
CORRECT   Gossage threw me a fastball.

It thus has less force than active voice. Similarly, clauses may be reduced to participial or prepositional phrases, and actually gain strength. (See also "Redundancy," above.)

Exercises

1. In *How to Write and Publish a Scientific Paper*, Robert Day suggests an amusing "Ten Commandments of Good Writing." Each sentence, however, violates the commandment it states. Restate the rules in correct English.

1. Each pronoun should agree with their antecedent.
2. Just between you and I, case is important.
3. A preposition is a poor word to end a sentence with.
4. Verbs has to agree with their subject.
5. Don't use no double negatives.
6. A writer mustn't shift your point of view.
7. When dangling, don't use participles.
8. Join clauses good, like a conjunction should.
9. Don't write a run-on sentence it is difficult when you got to punctuate it so it makes sense when the reader reads what you wrote.
10. About sentence fragments.

2. The following passage is choppy. Rewrite it into graceful style.

A great heat wave hit the United States. It happened during the summer of 1980. It soon turned into a disaster. It caused more than 1200 human deaths. It brought death and starvation to livestock. It caused crops to dry up in the fields. The human suffering could have been worse. Air conditioning probably saved thousands of lives.

The problem began in May, 1980. At that time, a hot air mass formed in the Pacific. It moved to the California coast. After that, the winds couldn't get through it. The winds usually flow from the Pacific across California. They cross the Southwest. They reach Texas. But there was no wind in Texas. So another hot mass formed there. This happened in mid-June. It was ignored at first. But it stayed. The heat spread. First it reached Oklahoma and Arkansas. Then it moved across Missouri and into Illinois. Finally the whole country felt the heat.

3.   Join or improve the following sentences through the use of parallelism. Use as few words as possible.

a. She sings competently. Sometimes she sings too loudly. Usually she sings feelingly.

b. Green plants need light. They also need water, and some people say, they need love.

c. Mike wrote his father. Carol wrote her mother. Sue wrote her sister.

d. Alice looks cheerful. So does Gail.

e. Please read Sam's manual. It's short. It contains useful details.

f. The students picked up their pens, they wrote, they erased, the teacher corrected them, and they rewrote.

g. The speaker stated his gratitude to the conference chairperson for her introduction, expressed appreciation to the audience for coming, and thanked the local arrangements committee for their hard work.

h. We need a president who is competent and will work hard.

i. Speaking casually, she told of her success as she sipped from her drink.

j. When the company goes bankrupt—if it goes bankrupt—I will need another job.

4.   Correct errors in the following sentences:

a. When singing, milk should not be drunk.

b. The work done as far as he concerned.

c. Not once I didn't make a mistake.

d. He refused permission, it was on account of the fact that he disapproved.

e. Bill said that a team of experts are coming.

f. Don't feed the animals, they don't like it.

g. I hadn't seen him since a few minutes ago.

h. It were our views that Hagerty not sign the checks.

i. He greeted a friend, picked up a drink, and Dr. Puhl was waving at him.

j. Alexis watched the horse moan and struggle, praying for the doctor's arrival.

5.   Shorten the following passage by removing wordiness.

It is the considered judgment of the court that there are two men in this case who have been irresponsibly negligent. The first of these two men is the one who sold the information of a secret nature, and the second is the one who willingly bought it. There is no reason to offer leniency in a case of such a nature, in consequence of which we therefore order full and complete payment of damages and the very maximum sentence, this being five years in prison.

Further Reading

Azar, Betty S. *Understanding and Using English Grammar.* Englewood Cliffs, N.J.: Prentice-Hall, 1981

Danielson, Dorothy, and Rebecca Hayden. *Using English: Your Second Language.* Englewood Cliffs, N.J.: Prentice-Hall, 1973

Dixson, Robert J. *Essential Idioms in English.* New York: Regents Publishing Co., 1971

Dixson, Robert J. *Graded Exercises in English.* New York: Regents Publishing Co., 1971

Hodges, John C., and Mary E. Whitten. *Harbrace College Handbook.* New York: Harcourt Brace Jovanovich, 1972

The Key to English ("Prepositions 1," "Prepositions 2," "Two-Word Verbs," etc). New York: Collier Macmillan International, 1964

Maclin, Alice. *Reference Guide to English: A Handbook of English as a Second Language.* New York: Holt, Rinehart and Winston, 1981

Index